ANTHONY ESOLEN

D0901616

*How the Church
Has Changed the World*

Publisher: Romain Lizé
Editor-in-Chief: Rev. Sebastian White, o.p.
Managing Editor: David Wharton
Iconography: Isabelle Mascaras
Layout: Julia Pateu
Cover: Gauthier Delauné
Production: Florence Bellot
Proofreading: Samuel Wigotow
Front cover: *The Holy Spirit* (detail of *The Adoration of the Mystic Lamb*, 1432),
Jan van Eyck (c. 1390-1441), Saint-Bavon Cathedral, Ghent, Belgium.
© akg-images.

Printed in March 2020 by Imprimerie Marquis, Canada
First edition: March 2020
Edition number: MGN20011
ISBN: 978-1-949239-30-0

ANTHONY ESOLEN

How the Church Has Changed the World

Volume II

January 2016 – December 2017

MAGNIFICAT

Paris • New York • Oxford • Madrid • Warsaw

CONTENTS

FOREWORD

At the end of Saint John's Gospel, after twenty-one chapters relating the miracles, teaching, and saving mysteries of the life of Our Lord, the Evangelist issues the following caveat: "There are many other things that Jesus did, but if these were to be described individually, I do not think the whole world would contain the books that would be written" (Jn 21:25).

The statement invites us to marvel at the plenitude of what our Savior accomplished two thousand years ago, in the course of the thirty-three years he dwelt among us. However, as the *Catechism* declares, even "when his visible presence was taken from them, Jesus did not leave his disciples orphans. He promised to remain with them until the end of time; he sent them his Spirit" (CCC 788; cf. Jn 14:18; 20:22; Mt 28:20; Acts 2:33). Accordingly, Catholic tradition refers to the *Christus totus*, the "whole Christ." Christ the Head, dwelling in glory, is one with and continues to act in his Body, the Church. How this is so has been the subject of many scholarly books. But "a reply of Saint Joan of Arc to her judges sums up the faith of the holy doctors and the good sense of the believer: 'About Jesus Christ and the Church, I simply know they're just one thing, and we shouldn't complicate the matter'" (Acts of the Trial of Joan of Arc; cf. CCC 795).

This second volume of essays by Professor Anthony Esolen offers twenty-four more examples of the redeeming presence of the Church in the world. You will see that the Church, far from fearing science and rational inquiry, has been the force behind some of our greatest advances. You will learn of statesmen who were moved by the faith in their courageous pursuit of a just social order. You will be inspired by the heroic efforts of missionaries, who traveled far and wide to draw more souls into the embrace of the Church. You will read of artists and thinkers who have left us some of civilization's greatest treasures. And you will see that saints and men and women of faith, far from having their freedom diminished or personalities muted by union with Christ and obedience to the Church, stand out as history's most free and vibrant figures.

Though we could never adequately express the ineffable goodness of Our Lord and his Church—please God, we will contemplate it for all eternity as members of the Church triumphant!—we may still do our part to make it better known while we remain *in via*. Thus, it is with great pleasure that we publish one more book exploring how the Church has changed the world.

Rev. Sebastian White, o.p.
Editor-in-Chief, Magnificat
Yonkers, New York
Solemnity of Saint Joseph, 2020

THE RECKONING OF THE TIMES

❧⟋⟍⟍❧

By the time you turn to this page, gentle reader, millions of people will have gathered in Times Square as usual to watch the great Secular Odometer turn from 99999 to 100000, as the new year begins, very like the old year, progressing on in the secular imagination toward some longed-for oasis of earthly delights, between the deserts of nothing before and nothing to come. Little do the feasters know that, were it not for Pope Gregory XIII, they would have arrived two weeks too late.

The Church teaches us that time springs from and returns to its origin in the providence of God the Creator. Or we might say that time is the rich soil wherein the wheat is sown for the harvest; or it is the arena for the heroic story of man's salvation, with its fixed center in Calvary, where Christ triumphant pierces the heart of hell with the cross. Or it is the meter of the epic of faith, as we fight the good fight or run the race to the finish. So the Church does not brush time aside. She sanctifies time and elevates it, giving us far more yearly feasts to celebrate than modern man, always a-bustle and always late, knows what to do with.

But she has also always wanted to get the time right. And here we run into difficulties.

When a baby boy was born to Augustine and Mary Washington on the shores of the Potomac River, they recorded his birthday as February 11, 1731. Many of us are familiar with the phenomenon of "losing" an hour or two as we travel by air from west to east, but that was nothing like what George Washington lost. For he was later to affirm, correctly, that he was born on February 22, 1732, giving Americans the date for the celebration of his birthday, and prompting the striking of the Washington quarter dollar in 1932, the year of its bicentennial.

What happened? Were his parents so far behind the times? It's one thing to be off by a day or two. But eleven? And a whole year?

A small error in the beginning

We turn then to Rome. The year is 1580, and a tireless old bulldog of a man, Gregory XIII, has succeeded Pope Saint Pius V to the Chair of Peter. Gregory founded or expanded about three hundred schools and universities. He appointed men like Saint Charles Borromeo to undertake a thorough reform of Catholic seminaries. He sent missionaries to all parts of the world, receiving emissaries from Japan to thank him for sowing the faith there. He founded the English college in Douai, France for the education of priests who then returned to their native land to celebrate

Mass in hiding and confer the sacraments, until such time as the priest-hunters of Queen Elizabeth should seize them and subject them to torture and a gruesome and protracted execution. It is said that Gregory sang the *Te Deum* when he heard about the Saint Bartholomew's Day massacre of Protestant Huguenots in Paris, but there was no Internet in those days, and all that the Pope knew of it was that a political revolt against a legitimate ruler had been put down. He wept when he learned at last what had really happened.

The times were also quite *literally* out of joint. If you ask a hundred people what a year is, you might get half of them to say that it is the time it takes for the earth to make one complete revolution about the sun. The next question is obvious. "How do you know when the earth has done that?"

"Well, you look at the calendar."

"And where did the calendar come from? If you didn't have a calendar, how would you know?"

Silence falls, and crickets chirp from the woods.

The sun has two apparent motions about the earth. The one is its daily journey from east to west. It is especially long in the summertime, when Mister Apollo the charioteer sweats at high noon, and his steeds long for their watering hole at the border of night.

The other movement is attributable to the tilt of the earth, of about twenty-three degrees. The tilt makes it so that the sun's path changes from day to day as the rotating earth moves in its yearly course. In England and North America, the sun rises higher and higher in its meridian as the days grow longer, until at one point it seems to "stop"—hence we have the word *solstice, sun-stop*. Then its noon is lower and lower in the sky, until at another point it stops again. We can measure our years according to the regular patterns of that path.

The problem is that the year is a little longer than 365 days. Julius Caesar tried to account for that by putting in "leap year" days for every fourth year, but that turned out to be a little too many. People began to notice it. Dante, in the Middle Ages, was well aware that the calendar had been lagging. Eventually, Beatrice says, the "neglected hundredths of your years" would cause spring to begin in January!

Not to worry, old ladies tending your flower gardens: that did not mean that snow would kill your daffodils, no more than Daylight Savings Time would fade your curtains. Days would be days and years would be years, but your computation would be off.

The keys to the calendar

So Gregory summoned one of his advisors, a German priest named Christopher Clavius (Christoph Klau), called the "Euclid of the 16th century." Clavius was that sort of Renaissance man who was really most prominent in the Middle Ages: born and raised in Bavaria, professor in Portugal, and papal mathematician and astronomer in Rome. Tycho Brahe and Johannes Kepler esteemed him highly, and he was a lifelong friend of Galileo. His voluminous works were translated into various languages; these included Chinese, so that his fellow Jesuits, such as his student Matteo Ricci, the great missionary to China, could take them to that land of clockmakers and stargazers and seekers of the Order of Heaven.

The most obvious need was to get rid of the ten "extra" days that had intruded. But Gregory and Clavius wanted more than calendrical duct tape. They wanted a solution that would, for all practical purposes, settle matters once and for all. That required excruciatingly precise astronomical observation and measurement and computation. What Clavius came up with was perfect, and was implemented in Catholic nations by papal decree in 1582.

That year, if your birthday fell between October 5 and 14 inclusive, well, you might as well have been born on February 30, because those ten dates for that year were cut out. But the problem would have arisen again, had not Clavius hit upon the notion of omitting leap-year days for three out of four *century* years. So we had a February 29 in 2000, divisible by 400, but there was none in 1900, and there will not be another one in a century year until 2400. That will keep our calendars in trim for the next thirty thousand years, if the Lord does not wind things up here sooner, as we hope he will.

Had Christendom not been divided, little George Washington would have been born on February 22 and not February 11 (you see, an eleventh extra day had wriggled in already). But for a long time the Protestant nations resisted adopting a "Catholic" calendar. That finally changed for England and her colonies in 1752—another year of vanishing dates—and now the Gregorian calendar is pretty much universal.

The true new year?

"But wait a moment," you say. "That explains the dates in February, but it doesn't explain the year."

Quite correct. You see, the convention of setting the beginning of the New Year as January 1 derives from Julius Caesar himself, but it wasn't the only candidate. Christians in England, for example, before the Norman Conquest in 1066 and then between 1155 and 1752, reckoned the New Year as beginning on March 25, the feast of the Annunciation. Other Christian countries counted Christmas, December 25, as beginning the new year. And why not?

For on that day when the angel appeared unto Mary, the Word was made flesh, and dwelt among us; and on that day nine months later we first beheld his glory, as he lay wrapped in swaddling clothes and lying in a manger.

And so the revelers in Times Square have a pope to thank, if they only knew it.

დ დ დ

A Map of Mankind

❧❦☙

An old man, dressed in a loose red robe, bows his head in respect, one scholar to another. His skin is a kind of dark amber, and his eyes glitter behind lids that sometimes make them look half shut. He is a storehouse of ancient lore. He knows the paths of the stars and the planets, what makes for a wise and useful minister, and what sacrifices are to be offered in honor of one's ancestors. He can tell the virtues of the good emperors and the vices of the bad. He is master of the multitudinous and labyrinthine pictograms of his written language.

"Honorable Father," he says, "I am ready to see the map."

The other scholar, a man in his prime, is dressed in the same manner, but he wears a cross around his neck. His flesh is permanently sun-darkened, and gleams with a tinge of bronze. His hair is black, with that wave in it that signifies *foreigner*. He responds to his visitor with the intimation of a smile, and rolls out a large parchment upon the table. It is covered with impossible shapes, like those of fabulous beasts, shaded in various colors, all of them lurking or peering beneath a grill of arcs and parallel lines.

"Here it is," says the young man.

They remain silent for a while. The old scholar touches the parchment here and there with his fingertips. "I do not see my land, Father."

"We are here, my good friend Pao," says the young man, pointing to a spot near the Great Sea. "All of this land, from the cold wasteland of the Mongol here, to Ton-kin in the south, and from the sea westward to the mountains of Tibet, all of this great land is yours."

"I had thought we were almost the whole world," said Pao, shaking his head a little sadly.

"Master Pao," the Jesuit Matteo Ricci replied, laying a hand upon the old man's shoulder, "that is a fond dream to which all men are prone."

Meeting people in Love

When Matteo Ricci traveled to the Far East as a missionary in 1580, he knew he had to learn everything he could about the Chinese culture, in order to bring them the Good News most effectively. He understood that the Chinese were an ancient and proud people, with long and venerable traditions. He spent several years in the Portuguese colony of Macao, mastering Mandarin Chinese, a language as different from any in Europe as it is possible to be. He had already studied mathematics and astronomy in Italy under the famous Father Christopher Clavius, with an eye to using those studies to earn the esteem and the friendship of the Chinese, who believed that the moral task of mankind on earth was to reflect the beautiful, silent Order of Heaven. In other words, Matteo Ricci was what we now would call an anthropologist, as were so many others among his brother missionaries.

I have heard people pride themselves on being "multicultural" who read at most two languages, and whose idea of culture seems to be limited to what comes out of the oven and what flag flies from the eaves. They have much to learn from the Catholic missionaries. You cannot bring the Good News to a people, or really any news at all, unless you *know them*, but to know human beings to the core you must love what is lovable in them, honor what is honorable, and forgive what is foolish or wicked. So the missionaries observed the peoples to whom they ministered, and their letters and diaries are invaluable sources of information.

But more than information. It is one thing to be aware that the Chinese believed that their land took up almost the whole globe, and to know that they would be surprised and dismayed to learn otherwise. It is quite another to be able to disentangle that pride and folly from their admirable sense of order and tradition, spanning many centuries. Matteo Ricci, like Junípero Serra, and Isaac Jogues, and Jean de Brébeuf, learned from the inside what the people were whom he loved. And we must insist upon the fact of this love.

Love that seeks truth

Consider what happens when the depth of Christian love is not there. Margaret Mead, the queen of anthropology, went to the South Seas and studied the mating habits of the natives, resulting in the too-influential and now-discredited *Coming of Age in Samoa*. She had something of a liberal agenda; the natives caught on to it, and played their cards accordingly. The people under the microscope flipped the lens the other way around. I'm not saying that Mead despised the Samoans; she liked them very much. But Father Ricci had to *love* the Chinese, with the charity that hopes all things, believes all things, and endures all things. Father Ricci had to love them with a love that would defy one disappointment after another, unto death. He was not martyred, but he would never return to his native land. He never enjoyed the accolades due to a celebrated scholar.

I think that the Catholic missionaries had to be most discerning, precisely because the articles of our faith are of ultimate concern. They could not simply say, "The people of China leave food offerings for their deceased ancestors, so they must be worshiping them as deities." Maybe they were, and maybe they weren't. Father Ricci determined that the most learned among them considered it an act of filial piety. Since they brought food to their elders in life, they thought that the best demonstration of their honor would be to "bring" food to them after their death. The common people, however, had mingled the practice with a good deal of superstition, and that, too, had to be taken into account.

Father Ricci sought out the wisest sages among the Chinese, and determined that the most ancient Chinese deity of all was the *T'ien-Chu Shih*-I—"heavenly Lord" or "Lord of heaven." That Lord was the one in whom all things had their origin, and whom all things in heaven and earth obeyed. So after long observation and careful study of the old texts, he wrote *The True Doctrine of God*, a short and brilliant catechism of the Catholic faith, filled with citations from the venerated words of such ancient wise men as Confucius and Mencius. For we believe that God does not leave any of his beloved people entirely in darkness.

Love of God, the bond of friendship

After many years of patient labor, Matteo Ricci was accorded the rarest of privileges. He, a mandarin from the West, was allowed entrance to the Forbidden City, the abode of the emperor himself. It was a momentous occasion.

For we are not talking about slick operators, buying land from indigenous peoples by paying them nuggets of glass, or rotting out their virtue by soaking them with firewater. Matteo Ricci came alone, with the best that his world had to offer, as a gift to the best of the people to whom he was both preacher and servant.

What a sight that must have been, in the early weeks of 1601, when Father Ricci, summoned at last by the Emperor Wan-Li himself, walked along the stately courtyards of the imperial grounds! I imagine him escorted by a parade of counselors and scholars and priests, while porters carry upon a litter the most fitting of gifts—maps and clocks and the astrolabe about which Father Ricci's teacher Clavius had written with so much precision and admiration. There before them rises the many-colored palace itself, its tiers of roofs curled in the style of the East, where dwelt the emperor, the North Star upon earth, whose duty was to rule his people with the same constancy as the North Star above ruled the heavens.

The man of God met a man who longed for God. Is that not the profoundest thing we can say about our fellow men, in whatever culture we may find them—that in the recesses of their hearts they long for God? If so, then only someone whose heart and mind are turned to God can ever really understand the hearts and minds of others.

I will not enter into the disputes that arose, the most bitter of them long after Father Ricci had died, between the Jesuits on one side and Dominicans and Franciscans on the other, regarding whether the mode of worship the Chinese Catholics had adopted was licit, or whether their continuing to honor their dead in the traditional way smacked too much of paganism. It is a tangled affair, ending in defeat for the Jesuit position. But Matteo Ricci has not been forgotten. The best of that noble culture, which the methodical and murderous Mao Zedong tried to sweep from the face of the earth, survives yet, and the moral seriousness of the Chinese, their natural piety, and their love of the beauty and order of the universe will someday, I firmly trust, find their fulfillment in Christ.

Yet another reason to turn in prayer to the east.

ↄ ↄ ↄ

The Joy of the Martyrs

❧⸙❧

Winston Smith, drinking oily gin in a drab little tavern called The Chestnut Tree, hears a song over the television that reminds him of something—what was it again?—that happened to him in a dungeon, in the bowels of the Ministry of Love:

> *Under the spreading chestnut tree*
> *I sold you and you sold me;*
> *There lie you and here lie we,*
> *Under the spreading chestnut tree.*

Yes, that was it. They had gotten inside him, prying open his heart. They had let loose the rats and spiders of his nightmares. They had made him betray Julia, the woman he loved. She had betrayed him also. Now all that was left of their love was like the cauterized knob of an amputated limb. His eyes welled up with tears, as the waiter brought him another bottle.

He had wanted to be a witness to the truth, but he had failed. If Big Brother said that two and two made five, then you had to think your way into agreeing with it. You had not merely to lie, but to believe your lie. Winston Smith was now too weary to go over it all again. They had won.

And now they jeered from the screen. Smith didn't know it, because poetry had been buried many fathoms deep under the sludge of all-in-all government, but the song was itself a parasite. A poet named Longfellow, many years before, had used that first line to honor a simple hard-working Christian man, a man of hope and integrity, who would sit among his boys on a Sunday in church, and hear his daughter singing. These were its first words:

> *Under a spreading chestnut tree*
> *The village smithy stands;*
> *The smith, a mighty man is he,*
> *With large and sinewy hands,*
> *And the muscles of his brawny arms*
> *Are strong as iron bands.*

But who can hold out against the father of lies, without the grace of God? George Orwell's defeated "hero" in *Nineteen Eighty-Four* had no faith.

Another dungeon

The scene is almost two thousand years ago. A fiery preacher from the desert sits in chains in a dank and vermin-ridden cell, beneath the palace of a puppet king. Years later, a man named John who once followed him would write that he, also named John—*God is gracious*—had come as a witness, to bear witness to the Light. The word he used was *martyria: witness, testimony*, and, in the end, what we know as *martyrdom.*

Sounds of the flute and tambourine, and dancing in sensuous abandon, reach him from above. Consider the contrast. In the halls of Herod Antipas we have wealth, good repute among the Roman occupiers, rich food and drink, and a young woman dancing before her stepfather, while her mother looks on, calculating. Below, the nearly naked John the Baptizer, and filth. It seems like all the world to nothing.

Not to the mother Herodias, though. Her husband, the brother-in-law with whom she is guilty of incest, fears John because he bears witness to the truth. She *hates* John for the same reason. So when the weakling king, ingratiated by the girl, promises her anything she desires, the girl, instructed by her mother, says, "Bring me the head of John the Baptizer on a platter." At which point truth and justice yield to face-saving and vengeance.

Down below, John hears the heavy door swing open, and knows it is time.

He need not have told a lie to save his life. All he had to do was to stop telling the truth. If you had collared a Roman soldier or even priest and held a knife to his throat, he'd have abjured the whole pantheon of pagan gods in a heartbeat.

Why, the gods themselves were traitors and liars when it suited them. Not the God of Israel.

What is truth?

It is a year later. The man for whom John came to witness, the true Light that enlightens everyone who comes into the world, is being tried for insurrection. The charges are baseless. They are lies. The Roman procurator, an intelligent but ruthless and cunning man, knows very well that they are lies.

"Are you a king?" he asks, not suppressing a smirk.

Again the contrast is stunning. The accused man has been beaten bloody. He owns nothing in the world but the clothes on his back. Behind the procurator stand all the colossal and bullying symbols of Roman authority.

"Are you the king of the Jews?"

The man replies. He is a king, but his kingdom is not of this world. "So then you are a king?" says the procurator, wavering between contempt and fear.

He had been hoping for a decent night's rest. The last thing he'd wanted was to have to deal with these Jews and their mad religion, their mad belief in the one true God. He had thought he could dispose of this matter without having to think. Thought is dangerous. Thought can bring you to the door of truth. There are all kinds of reasons for wanting that door to stay shut. Men cannot endure the light.

"You say that I am a king," says the accused. "For this reason I was born and came into the world," he says, speaking the common language of the east, "*hina martyreso tei aletheiai*," that he might be a witness, a *martyr*, to the truth.

Without truth to witness to, there is no martyrdom. Without God to give us the grace and the courage, there is no martyrdom, because on our own we have no strength to hold out against the lie.

"What is truth?" asked Pontius Pilate, washing his mind before he washed his hands.

We are martyrs to the Resurrection

It is a few weeks later, at Solomon's portico. Many thousands of Jews from all over the world have come to Jerusalem to celebrate the feast of Pentecost, the fiftieth day after Passover—the great jubilee day. It is a feast of gratitude and rejoicing.

But a sudden wind has swept the city, and people are shouting and crying out in their many tongues—What has happened? What is going on?

A man of broad shoulders, in the ordinary clothing of a workman, stands forth on a balcony above. He is speaking.

There was a night when he did not speak. His master had been arrested and put on trial for his life. On that night this man, Simon, christened "Rock" by the master in one of his moments of sublime command or irony or both, had refused to witness to the truth. "I tell you," he snapped at the serving woman, trying to muffle his Galilean accent, "I don't know the man!" Cunning strategy, that. But Jesus glanced his way, and "Rock," Peter, left the area and wandered into the night, weeping bitterly.

Now he stands and speaks. "Men of Israel, do not be amazed," he cries. For the promised Messiah had come, and they had put to death the Lord of life, but God has raised him from the dead, "and of this we are *martyres*!"

Thousands of repentant sinners would be baptized on that day, says Saint Luke. But Peter knew what kind of final witness, what *martyrdom*, awaited him. The risen Lord had told him there would come a time when men would bind him and take him where he did not want to go.

He would be crucified upside down, on the Vatican hill, outside the walls of Rome.

God is the ultimate witness

The history of the Christian faith is the story of that great cloud of martyrs which surrounds us all. Some of them, like Saint Sebastian, his body riddled with arrows, died violent deaths at the hands of Roman persecutors. Others journeyed into pagan lands, like Saint Boniface, and toiled to bring the truth, knowing that eventually it would cost them their lives. Others, like Saint Damien of Moloka'i, accepted a permanent exile from their homelands—for Damien, imprisonment in a colony of lepers, to bring to his fellow men healing in body and soul.

Sometimes the father of lies is not so bloody. Then our martyrdom may be the laughter and scorn of the world; for who but a fool would live in the alleys of Calcutta, or who but someone obsessed and mad would shut himself up in a cave in Egypt, to spend his life in prayer?

But in the end the same question is posed to everyone. And it is a question the world never has really understood. The world may kill, and often does kill, for glory or wealth or ambition or vengeance or fear. *But to set your very life on the line for truth, to be slaughtered like a lamb for truth*—well, what the pagan world got from Socrates, the history of the Church has gotten from hundreds of thousands of ordinary men and women and even children, and in our supposedly enlightened time more than ever.

These bear witness to the world, against the world, *for the sake of the world*, and the world, because its ways are evil, stops up its ears against the truth that would set it free.

None of this could ever come to pass, except by faith in the ultimate martyr, the God who will stand witness for us.

"*Martyro ego*," says the Lord to John at the end of his mysterious and resplendent vision: *He shall bear witness* to all who hear the words of truth.

ༀ ༀ ༀ

THEY BROUGHT
THEIR SICK TO HIM

❦

The preacher stands before the crowds, sparing no one's complacency. "You array your bodies and your homes with luxury," he cries, "but the most glorious creature that God ever made, your fellow man, you allow to go in tatters! Hear what the rich man in the parable says. He will pull down his barns and erect a great granary, a monument to his pride, and then he will live at his ease. Fool! That very night the Lord will require of him his life."

His name is Basil, "king." That name is both apt and deeply ironic. You'd never look upon his spare form and think of royalty. For clothing he owns but a cloak and sandals. He lives mainly on bread and water. But by his very poverty and piety he gains an authority over his congregation that kings can never know, in all their regalia and their trailing retinues of favorites and flatterers.

For Basil, poverty was not merely a social problem, to be addressed by distant and impersonal measures. The poor man who borrows as a last resort, and who then scrambles under his bed when he hears his creditor's knock on the door—that is your brother. The boy who survives in the street by stealing, he is your own son. Other preachers might be content with general principles of Christian charity. Not Basil.

The Mass ends, and the people return to their homes in the swarming city of Caesarea, named for the emperor Augustus on his death in 14 A.D. For the Roman armies had reduced the vast high plateau of Cappadocia to the liberty of a Roman province. To the north, the great River Halys bends on its course to the Black Sea. To the south a great snowy volcanic cone, Mount Argaeus, rises more than a mile and a half above the surrounding country.

If you are poor or sick in this land, so much the worse for you. It's not the honey-sweet land of the Greek isles, near to the swell of the wine-dark sea. It is far inland, brutally hot in summer, icy in winter. The harvests have been poor, and the people are hungry. And the armies of the Arian emperor Valens have been doing bloody work. In that place, at that time, Saint Basil came to a decision.

"We need a new city," he said.

Theirs is the kingdom of heaven

"Beggars and strangers come from Zeus," went the old Greek proverb, for the gods would come down to put arrogant men to the test, showing up at their gates with a walking stick and in rags. There was no sense that the poor should be *loved*. Hospitality is one thing, but love is quite another. Maybe we can translate the proverb in this way: "People who cringe and who don't belong here might be sent by that master of justice—and cunning. We'd better watch out."

But Jesus the journeying preacher from dusty Palestine had changed all that forever, at least for those who profess to follow him. "Blessed are the poor," he said, "for theirs is the kingdom of heaven." And if you're too rich to beg, your well-laden camel might find entry into its gates a bit tight. The pagans understood, deep down, that there was something at least uneasy about riches. Menelaus, in the *Odyssey*, is a very rich man—but not much of a man. Socrates didn't own much, but he did cadge dinners at the homes of his rich young patrons. Yes, the pagans understood it, somewhere, somehow, just as pagans nowadays understand it. Such understanding is cheap.

Basil had long been doing the work of Christian charity. Here's how his dear friend, Saint Gregory of Nazianzen, described it:

> "He gathered together the victims of the famine with some who were but slightly recovering from it, men and women, infants, old men, every age which was in distress, and obtaining contributions of all sorts of food which can relieve famine, set before them

basins of soup and such meat as was found preserved among us, on which the poor live. Then, imitating the ministry of Christ, who, girded with a towel, did not disdain to wash the disciples' feet, using for this purpose the aid of his own servants, and also of his fellow servants, he attended to the bodies and souls of those who needed it, combining personal respect with the supply of their necessity, and so giving them a double relief."

See how they love one another!

How to bring personal care to the thousands who needed it—that was the problem. Nothing like it had been done in the history of the world. *A new city* indeed was needed.

So Basil acquired some land outside of Caesarea, and there he began to build.

The ancients had no true hospitals for everyone. The Romans had built infirmaries for veteran soldiers, or for the valued slaves of the wealthy, but in general, if you were a sick man and had no patron, you were out of luck. You might go to the temple of the healer-god, Asclepius, and pray that he might lift the curse from your body. That was about it.

Christians, however, had been commanded to tend the sick, in body and spirit, and this duty fell most of all upon the bishop, the priests, and in particular the servants, that is, the deacons. The bishop's very home was to be open to all travelers. That was the command, and the practice lived up to it. The apostate emperor Julian famously wrote, in envy, that the Christians put his fellow pagans to shame, because they did a better job *taking care of pagans* than the pagans themselves did!

The Christians did so in homage to Christ the Healer, of whom Asclepius was but a shadowy allegory, as Saint Justin had said almost two hundred years before. Jesus had gone about Galilee and Judea healing the sick, and his disciples and Apostles would do the same, and if someone was dying, said Saint James, then the priest should lay his hands upon him and anoint him, and confer healing, if not of the body, then of the sin-sick soul. We remember the Samaritan in Jesus' parable, who went down into the ditch by the roadside to take up the man who had fallen among thieves, to clean his flesh with wine and oil, and to bind up his wounds with his own hands.

Hands—not mere money, but hands.

The city rises

Basil called it the *Ptochotrephion*, the House for Care of the Poor, but others soon called it the *Basiliad*, or simply the *New City*.

Imagine separate buildings for those who were afflicted by the plague, for those who were recovering, for the lepers whom no self-respecting pagan would go near, for women in childbirth, and for people nearly starved with the famine. Imagine hospices for travelers, and chapels for all of us wayfarers on the road to the last things.

Imagine schools—especially shops where a young man with no money and no prospects might learn a gainful trade, to be a mason, a tanner, a potter, a carpenter. Imagine monks, hundreds of them, for whom this entire city is their monastery. One monk washes the purulent sores of a dying man. Another is showing a boy how not to gouge the wood with the plane. Another plies his hoe in a large field of vegetables. Another brings the Body of Christ to a child too sick to move. Another digs a grave. All of them are working and praying.

In his eulogy for Basil's requiem Mass, Saint Gregory Nazianzen praised this wonder of love, greater in real glory than "seven-gated Thebes… and the pyramids, and the immeasurable bronze of the Colossus," and all those other wonders of the world, which gained their founders nothing but a little brief fame. "Go forth a little way from Caesarea," he said, "and behold the new city, the storehouse of piety, the common treasury of the wealthy, in which the superfluities of their wealth, yes, and even their necessaries, are stored, in consequence of [Basil's] exhortations, freed from the power of the moth, no longer gladdening the eyes of the thief, and escaping both the emulation of envy, and the corruption of time: where disease is regarded in a religious light, and disaster is thought a blessing, and sympathy is put to the test." Even the lepers are welcome there, "composers of piteous songs, if any of them have their voice still left to them."

If only we had one now

Such were the *hospitals*, which the Church bequeathed to the world. And now our sick are cared for in buildings twenty stories high, with medicines and machines that Saint Basil could never have imagined. Yet I have a fond hope that someday, amid the un-music of monitors, within the icy white walls, beyond the reach of accountants and executive officers, something of the human, something of the love that touches the soul of man, will return. We all must die, medicine or no. It would be a good thing at least to die among friends, strengthened and cheered by good men of God, and given that last sweet nourishment for the journey; to be with Christ, to receive Christ, on the way to Christ.

$$\text{ } \quad \text{ } \quad \text{ }$$

MELODIES EVERLASTING

❧❧❧❧❧

Necessity is the mother of invention, they say, but in the history of the Church it has rather been zeal and charity. If I am going to evangelize a pagan people who live partly by herding sheep and partly by killing their distant kin and taking their property, I will have to learn how to speak to them and how to teach them the doctrines of the faith, and eventually that will mean bringing them into the world of books. So in one sense it was a necessity that the monks who traveled north to the German tribes had to find a way to adapt the Roman alphabet to the sounds of their languages, using combinations of letters that were utterly impossible to civilized speakers of Latin. Consider, just for Anglo-Saxon, such "barbaric" ways of beginning a word as *hl, hr, hw, wr, wl*, and *cn*, not to mention new characters for such odd sounds as that of *th* in *this* and *a* in *that* and *w* in *will*. Why, so strange to the ear were the Slavic tongues that Saints Cyril and Methodius had pretty much to invent a new alphabet altogether. They *had to* do these things, if they were to evangelize. But who if not Love himself had sent them among barbarians to begin with?

So they dealt with speaking and reading. But what about that exalted form of expression known as *singing*?

Where are the songs of yesteryear? Aye, where are they? The ancient Greeks and Romans had their sacred songs, and their love songs, and war songs, and drinking songs. The Old Testament is filled with songs, including that most ravishing Song of Songs, redolent of eastern spices and dropping with honey. Do we have these ancient songs? We have their words. We do not have the melodies. The "alphabet" of music hadn't been invented. Oh, there was a lot of musical theory, and even musical mathematics. There were the "modes" with their Greek names, and customs regarding the kinds of rhythm that were fit for each. But, in the end, to learn music was like learning to recite poetry, among people who have no letters. It was to hear and repeat, to hear and repeat.

Hippocrates famously said that the physician's art was long, and life was short. He might have said the same thing about getting by heart the chants of the Church.

Songs for the year, songs for the ages

They weren't just three or four, those chants of the Church. Consider all of the prayers for every Sunday and feast day in the year. Consider the special hymns for morning and evening, for the Eucharist, for the penitential seasons, for the dedication of a church, or for the burial of the dead. Consider the 150 Psalms, which monks all across Europe would chant during a single week at the most. What can you do with all of those melodies?

You had three choices. First, you could shrug and say that whatever they were singing at Saint Gall need have nothing to do with what they sang at Monte Cassino. Let everyone sing *ad libidinem*. What difference does it make? Why should God care? But that violates the spirit of the liturgy itself, which demands that we give God our best, as did that first good shepherd Abel, and not any old mildewed ear of corn, as did Cain. It also betrays the universality of the Church. It is deeply comforting—strengthening—to know that when you sing the *Victimae paschali* at Easter, you are joining your voice with men and women and children the world over, in a harmony of worship and word and melody.

The second choice is what had prevailed for centuries. You could take the trouble to learn every one of the melodies by heart, and to teach them to others *exactly* as you learned them. That meant that to be a cantor at a church, you had to study under a master for two or three years. The problem with this, besides the sheer excruciating labor, is that eventually people make mistakes, and original melodies can be corrupted or lost altogether. For, unlike poetry, the music of the chant was "horizontal," not divided into easily recognized portions, and not structured by regularly recurring devices such as rhyme or the strict meters of Greek and Latin verse. The music was subordinate to the words and their meaning, and so could most delightfully "wander" accordingly, all while remaining within the range of an ordinary human voice.

Then there was a third choice.

The pope reads a song

"I've called you, Brother Guido," says an old man seated upon a chair of authority, "to witness for myself the admirable discovery you have made."

The monk approaches. He is unsteady on his feet. One summer in mosquito-ridden Rome has ruined his health. Besides, he has had his share of trials and disappointments.

"Holiness," says the monk, "my enemies have brought me no end of trouble. Envy is a worse plague than malaria, and you see what that has done to me."

"Have no fear, my son. Bring me your famous book."

It is an antiphonary. Above the words in Latin, Pope John XIX saw what looked like a monastic grill, placed on its side: four parallel lines, extending from one end of a page to the other. One of the lines was marked in yellow. The monk said that that denoted the sound we call C. A red line marked F. A series of black marks—we now call them *notes*—were scattered not only along the lines but in the spaces between the lines. There were also some thin vertical lines to connect one note with another above it or below it. Sometimes one note was followed by another in the same position, but most of the time the music was ascending or descending. The trick was to find a way to fix how great the intervals were.

The monk now warmed to his task. "I've written that to learn music without a staff is like being down a well without a rope. Here is how the staff works." And he demonstrated to the pontiff what the notation meant, and how you could "see" the intervals we call a third or a fourth or a fifth.

We've all heard of the burst of meaning that came upon the blind and deaf girl, Helen Keller, when under the spout of a well-pump it suddenly came to her that the finger-signs her teacher tapped into her hand meant "water." I imagine that something like her astonishment struck Pope John.

"I can read this!" he gasped, running his finger along the staves and singing the verses softly. "I can read it, without a singing master!"

A magnificent invention

Brother Guido of Arezzo was soon welcomed back to the monastery whence he had been driven, and his invention spread across the continent. He wrote that the old method was like being a blind man who had to be led by hand. It was all right, he said, for boys who were just beginning, but frustrating for those who had progressed in the art. When he taught his boys the new method, some of them "could in three days sing a chant with ease, which under the old method they could have not have accomplished in many weeks."

The method was more subtle than I can describe here. For one thing, Guido had to distinguish among different pitches of the same fundamental note, so that the boys singing soprano would have their A, and the men singing alto and tenor would have theirs. "Just as there are seven days" of creation, said Guido, so there are exactly seven "voices" or notes, designated by the familiar series of letters A, B, C, D, E, F, and G; the next note returning to A. He had to describe which notes were separated by a full tone, and which by a semi-tone; the "black keys" of western music, so to speak, had not been invented yet (except for that wonderfully sweet B flat). He described then how his method worked with the seven modes—two of which we would recognize as our major and minor scales.

Those are important details, but the main thing is that for the first time in the history of the world, there was a reliable way to hand music along from one generation to the next, or from people in Italy to people in Ireland at the edge of the world. Mozart once wrote that he would have given all his work for the fame of having composed the Gregorian Preface. He could never have uttered that pious exclamation—the Preface could never have endured, nor could he have composed his own work—had it not been for the zeal of the musical monk from Arezzo.

Boethius in Prison

⦿⟑⟨⦿⟩⟑⦿

It was the year 524 since the birth of the Incarnate Word. It was 1,277 years since the mythical founding of the City. It was forty-eight years since the last emperor of Rome in the west, a boy with the bitterly ironic name Romulus Augustulus, was "advised" to quit his throne and become a harmless monk, while the true rulers, Germans, took over.

Severinus paced in his cell, waiting for the voices to go away. Never had their accents struck his ear as quite so barbarous as they did now, guttural and crude. *Se reiks…wil…frijonds dauths… the emperor wants his friend dead*, and they laughed and slapped one another on the back for a job well done.

Why had he meddled with politics, anyway? He was more than a scholar "at heart." He was a scholar through and through, the greatest scholar of his century. He was an expert in the Greek philosophies going back to Plato. He was a profound theologian who wrote upon the Trinity. He was a mathematician and a theorist of music. He would dearly have wished to do nothing but read and write, in his villa—especially to realize his old ambition, to show the world that the visions of Plato and Aristotle were one.

But he never enjoyed that retirement. Severinus loved his country, or what was left of it, and he believed he could serve loyally both Rome and the heretic warlord Theodoric, his master. At least he could try. He was too much of a Roman not to try. He could work to preserve the residual liberties of the Senate, to affirm the authority of the true emperor in Constantinople, to protect the orthodox Catholic Church from the new Arian overlords, and somehow find time to shore up against the storm the fragments of a world in shambles.

Theodoric was a capable administrator and, for a Goth, a humane ruler. But he felt his inferiority. When the enemies of Severinus, traitors and perjurers and thieves, accused the scholar of engaging in a plot with the Senate, Theodoric condemned him to death. The Senate, a pack of ingratiating cowards, joined in. It was all a lie.

And now, Severinus thought, his reputation was ruined, and his life was over. Nor could he expect the solemn and quick execution proper to a Roman citizen. The Goths had other means than the headsman's ax.

This is what they would do: they would soak a leather thong in hot vinegar to stretch it, and then they would manacle Severinus and fasten the thong around his forehead. Over the course of two or three days the thong would shrink, crushing the skull and penetrating the brain. That was the death awaiting him.

One last gift

But Theodoric was not wholly heartless. He gave Severinus a precious gift: pen and ink and papyrus. With them, from the few days he had left, Severinus, whom we know as Boethius, gave to the world his greatest work, one that we cannot dismiss as airy speculation detached from the mire and blood of human suffering. It would be, second to the Bible, the most translated work in the Christian west for the next eleven hundred years. We can esteem it for its power of expression and clarity of thought, in alternating sections of prose and the last really great poetry of ancient Rome. But those of us who have once been moved by *The Consolation of Philosophy* love it best for its courage and wisdom, and its assertion of the never-failing providence of the Father.

Reader, have you ever feared that your life was falling apart about you? Imagine then Severinus alone in his cell, lamenting in these words, in verse:

Why, my friends, did you so often boast of my good fortune? The man who has fallen never did stand upon a firm step.

At which point, he says, "It seemed that I saw a woman of reverend countenance, standing high above me, with flashing eyes and quicker vision than is common to mankind," young in feature, yet so old that she could not belong to his own age. Her stature was as impossible to fix as were her years. Sometimes she seemed to be of ordinary human height, and yet sometimes, when she lifted herself to her full stature, she might pierce the heavens themselves. She is old and ever fresh, human and yet in contemplation more than human. Her name is Lady Philosophy—Lady Love of Wisdom.

And *her* last gift to Severinus will be the consolation that truth affords.

In prison, but free

"*O stelliferi conditor orbis*," cries the prisoner, "O Creator of the star-bearing wheel"—why should we look to the heavens and see the beauty of law and orderly motion, but look to the earth and sinful mankind and see confusion?

We expect perhaps that Lady Love of Wisdom will soothe Severinus by letting him rest his head upon her bosom, as she strokes his hair and says, "You're right, my darling, so right." And what good would that do? It would be like giving a drink to the condemned man, to soak his sorrows in wine and forgetfulness. She does no such thing. "But as for you," she says, friendly and calm, "how far you are from your fatherland—not driven into exile, but wandering away, or if you have been driven, you yourself have done the driving!"

She begins with the crucial question. Does he believe that the world is governed, or is it a matter of mere chance? This question is all or nothing. Is the ultimate principle of the world order, or is it disorder and chaos? But how can we even call chaos a "principle," since it would be the antithesis of law, and thus could never begin anything?

"I could never imagine," says Severinus, thinking of the sun and the moon, the planets and the stars, "that such certain motions would be caused by heedless chance. I know that God the Creator presides over his work, nor shall the day come that can thrust me from the truth of that judgment."

In the midst of his fear and disappointment, and near despair, Severinus cries out, Not nothing! From this one spark of the intellect, Lady Love of Wisdom will kindle again in his soul the vision of immutable truth: God never abandons the citizens of his country.

The things that men pursue as if they were the whole good, things in the gift of wheel-spinning Fortune—yes, reader, the Wheel of Fortune makes its first appearance here—deceive us. It's not that wealth, power, fame, honor, and pleasure are bad things in themselves. They are *partial* things. We seek the whole good, the One who unites in himself, not by conglomeration but in a single essence, all that is good in these other things. The pursuit of happiness leads inevitably to disappointment and failure, says Lady Love of Wisdom, if it aims at only the part and not the whole. Thus do vicious men suffer the punishment in the very vice they practice, because they lose by it not just some victory in a footrace, but the aim and end of all human action.

But virtuous men are tried by God, for their good. God protects some who are weak by giving them only good fortune. He gives to some virtuous men the most terrible trials, that they may emerge victorious and shine as exemplars for their fellow men. He gives an easy life to some vicious men, that penury may not prompt them to crimes even worse; or he may, as severe punishment, withhold from them the reversals that might prompt them to repent. We do not know and cannot know what God may intend in his special providence for any individual.

"O you who govern the world with perpetual reason," sings Lady Love of Wisdom in the most famous poem of the work, begging God to inspire them by the beauty of his creation and the moral order:

Shine forth in thy splendor! For thou art the se-rene, thou the tranquil repose for pious men, and to look upon thee is the goal of all: Thou art their beginning, their inspiration, their guide, their way, and their end.

A timely gift for us

Boethius was the one man most responsible for bequeathing classical learning to the west, to survive the Dark Ages to come, until the Medieval world should burst forth in its wonderful light. Yet I think that the *Consolation* may be meant for us now in a special way. The barbarians are back. Humane learning is forgotten or despised. The Church is buffeted, while the gargoyles of the age caper and make mouths and laugh. I imagine that the Gothic keepers of the jail cracked their jokes too.

Anicius Manlius Severinus Boethius kept faith to the end. No one honors or even remembers his accusers; but the Catholics of Lombardy honored and remembered him straightaway: Saint Severinus. His bones rest in the cathedral of Pavia, where the bones of Saint Augustine also lie.

It is better for us to wait with that man in his cell than to enjoy all of the vast earth among men gone mad, quite mad. God give us the courage to do so!

ෆ ෆ ෆ

JOURNEYING TO THE TRUTH

⊷•⊶❦⊷•⊶

In the spring of 1933, a young man nearing the prime of life, exceptionally handsome and an artist with words, picked up a train ticket from Moscow to Kiev, ducking the Soviet security system. He was one of three journalists the Soviets had chosen to tell the world that everything was coming up milk and honey in their farms. For Stalin had rounded up all the resistant landowners in the fertile Ukraine and sent them to the tundra or had them shot. He intended to turn all their farms into collectives, because according to the Marxist theory, that was the thing to do. It had to work. It also served to rub out his enemies, crush the Ukrainians, and establish the name he had given himself—"Steel"—as a synonym for cold, inflexible terror.

By temperament and upbringing, the writer was suspicious of all the posturing of those who are considered great in the world. He saw through the swagger. He knew that Stalin was lying. He also knew that everyone else in the Soviet Union knew it. The question was not, "Are millions of people dying of hunger in Ukraine?" They were. They had eaten their seed corn. They had eaten

their cattle. There were credible reports of canni-
balism. An "experimental" farm run by Germans
had to employ five men whose only work, day in
and day out, was to bury the dead peasants who
had come there begging for food. Many millions
would starve.

So the young Malcolm Muggeridge went to
see for himself. Many years later he made light of
the danger. "It was actually pleasant," he said of
the Pullman coach that offered "endless glasses of
hot tea." He was not new to human disasters. He
had been a British civil servant in India, and had
lived through an epidemic of cholera. But, said
he, "the novelty of this particular famine, what
made it so diabolical, is that it was not the result
of some catastrophe like a drought or an epidemic. It was the deliberate creation of a bureaucratic
mind": the breadbasket of Europe, turned into a
wilderness. He vowed to tell the truth.

Others had not. Walter Duranty, writing for
The New York Times, won a Pulitzer for his cream-
puff reportage of the communist paradise. Duranty
was an amiable companion, said Muggeridge, but
also "the greatest liar of any journalist I have ever
met," and *that* took some doing. Muggeridge was
an agnostic, and by no means the most virtuous
man in the room. But he loved truth. So he re-
ported for the British *Guardian*: "The fields are
neglected and full of weeds; no cattle are to be

seen anywhere, and few horses; only the military and [Communist party officials] are well fed, and the rest of the population obviously starving, obviously terrorized."

Did Malcolm Muggeridge win a prize for his courageous reporting? Hardly. He lost his job—and, what's more, *he knew he would*. If there were rainbow banners in those days, they were all for Stalin, the darling of the secular Left. Several years later, when Stalin joined hands with Hitler, Muggeridge allowed himself to imagine "the Dean of Canterbury having a momentary doubt as to whether Stalin really would go on building the Kingdom of Christ." The moment passed. He knew that the western intelligentsia would be like dope addicts returning to the next dose.

A humble woman in Calcutta

It is more than three decades later. Our journalist has seen the "sheer imbecility of the kingdom of heaven on earth, as envisaged by the most authoritative and powerful voices of our time." A mad spree of wealth and toys, people stupefied by television and sex, "happiness in as many colors as there are pills." Nor was he overwhelmed by the totem of our day. "Towards any kind of scientific mumbo-jumbo," he wrote, "we display a credulity which must be the envy of African witch-doctors." But Muggeridge did not shroud his soul in satire. The cynic hates falsehood, but he does not love the truth. Muggeridge continued to seek, and that made him, again and again, to turn to the words and the person of Jesus, *more alive now* than we who walk the earth. And still Muggeridge did not believe in the Resurrection.

But this love for Jesus drew him to Calcutta, where a little wizened old Albanian nun was toiling in obscurity, loving the destitute and the dying, people afflicted with leprosy and gangrene, children reduced to sticks, human refuse. Her name was Mother Teresa.

Yes, it was the same journalist who made Mother Teresa known to the world, first through a documentary and then through his book *Something Beautiful for God*. "In a dark time," he wrote, "she is a burning and shining light; in a cruel time, a living embodiment of Christ's Gospel of love; in a Godless time, the Word dwelling among us, full of grace and truth." Muggeridge donated all of the book's proceeds to Mother Teresa's work. The two became very dear friends.

What an unlikely friendship that might seem, on the face of it! But consider. Muggeridge had seen the parade of the "great" come and go. The worst were devils in human form; even the best, a Churchill or an Eisenhower, were, in his eyes, at least half humbug. He was a world traveler, while the nun's daily rounds were confined to that dreadful urban hole. He could have rolled his eyes and smiled to himself at her simple faith. He did not. Here was truth, in action.

Muggeridge and Mother Teresa continued to correspond by letter. She prayed for him ceaselessly, admonishing him, advising him to become like a little child, and to overcome the finite—the all-too-visible failings of the Church upon earth—with the infinite. Finally, in 1982, at the age of seventy-nine, Malcolm Muggeridge was baptized a Roman Catholic, he and his wife Kitty.

"I thirst"

Yet maybe they were united by something else, something that strikes the world with terror.

Malcolm Muggeridge tried to expose the liar Stalin to a world gone merry for its latest substitutes for Jesus and the Kingdom of God. The world would not listen. Then he brought to the world's never-very-keen attention the greatest Christian missionary of a century awash in blood and gin. The world seemed to listen for a while. But now that both he and she have passed on to the judgment of their Maker, the world has had second thoughts.

The world—that same world that found much wisdom in millions of copies of Mao's Little Red Book, the world that never met a tyrant it didn't like, the world fooled by ideas so brutally stupid and unreal that only intellectuals can believe them and dictators enforce them—*that world*, with its knowing smirk, now says that Mother Teresa perhaps was not a saint, and that Muggeridge sort of made her up.

Thousands of Missionaries of Charity are scattered across the world, doing work that no one else will do, and accompanying that work with gentle hands and loving smiles that no one else will give. They are real, and the people they tend are real. But Mother Teresa called abortion the greatest sin of our age, and Muggeridge was her apostle, Muggeridge who dared to tear the curtain from the Soviet vaudeville show, and who never ceased to laugh at the modern world and its bluster, its glamour and pomp and empty promises. So they must be slandered. The world knows better.

It seems to me a battle of drinkers, this. We know from her diary that Mother Teresa was given a locution from Christ: his terrible words upon the cross. "I thirst," said he. He still does. He is still where we have put him, on the black cross against a blank sky, thirsting, the longing that is more urgent than hunger, thirsting in love for souls in danger of loss. He is the Savior who promises living waters to all who thirst, and who gives his blood as wine for his enemies, yearning to entice them with its taste, the taste of purity, holiness, and truth. It is a heady liquor. To Mother Teresa it was given to share in that thirst of Christ.

And somehow, somewhere in his long life, by the grace of God the agnostic journalist was given a taste of the wine. The world slakes its thirst elsewhere. It has made itself drunk on ditch water. Let us not do so. For Jesus, we know, is an excellent host. He saves the best wine for last.

 භ භ භ

Ramon Llull, Missionary to the Muslims

Ramon sat upon the shore, looking south-ward upon the broad and sunlit sea. Palm trees with their dark green and glossy fronds rose high above him, their roots sent deep into the gray volcanic stone that is the island of Majorca. A fire was burning within him.

"What are you doing here, Ramon?" asked a cool and knowing voice at his side. "Are you thinking about one of your mistresses? Composing a new song, my fine young troubadour?"

"No, I am not composing a song. My heart is troubled."

"Then I've come in good time to set you at ease," said the voice. "Come back with me to Palma. There is a young lady who cannot sleep, all because of you. Are you worried about your wife? She knows, too. She is no fool. Come with me and live life as the world lives it. Bring your lute and sing for love."

Ramon felt at once how easy it would be to lie back and love with the half-hearted love that the world knows, for things that fall away, one day like the next, until death ends the song. But there came into his mind the vision that troubled him. On five days, one after another, he had seen love in the person of the crucified Christ, suspended in space before him. The blood from his pierced heart and hands trickled upon him, and his soul was stirred to new life.

"I have never loved," said Ramon.

"You are a fool," said the voice, grown suddenly cold.

"I will be a fool for love," said Ramon.

"You have your freedom now," said the voice, as if with a smile or a sneer. "You are the seneschal of the king. You are handsome and intelligent, and there is hardly a lady's chamber door that you cannot penetrate with your music. Sing, and it shall be opened unto you."

"I will be the slave of love," said Ramon.

"Tell us, Fool! What is love?" He answered: "Love is that which throws the free into bondage, and gives liberty to those who are in bonds." And who can say whether love is nearer to liberty than to bondage?

Blessed Ramon Llull would write those words, in a remarkable book of poetic meditations, one for each day of the year. But that was yet to come.

The sword of love

Ramon Llull became a lay Franciscan, inspired by the story of that most amiable of God's

fools, the high-living young poet and sing-
er Francis who gave up everything to marry his
Lady Poverty, and who strode unarmed before
the Sultan to persuade him of the truth of the
Christian faith. Everywhere Ramon looked, there
was the sea, and beyond the sea, the followers of
Mohammed, learned, wealthy, and implacable.
His father had been a Crusader. I will not join the
easy despisers of the Crusader knights, who often
impoverished themselves and left their homelands
never to return, to win back the Holy Land for
the faith. Yet after more than a hundred years,
what had they gained for all their effort? A narrow
strip of land between the desert and the sea, surrounded by enemies.

Ramon decided he would fight with a different sword, the sword of love.

He did not adopt the slack modern habit of
the shrug, seeing no difference where there was
all the difference in the world. The religion of
Mohammed was radically deficient. It was, however, in possession of *some of the truth* about God.
So Ramon Llull decided he would conduct a powerful attack against Islam by employing the truths
of Islam itself. He would conduct this attack *in
love, and love would be also its intellectual center.*

That meant that he would have to learn what
the Muslims knew. So he spent his next nine
years, mostly in Majorca, learning Arabic and

immersing himself in the works of such great Arabic philosophers and theologians as Averroës, Avicenna, and Al-Ghazali. His friend Saint Raymond of Peñafort encouraged him in this, as he had also encouraged another young scholar, a man from Aquino, named Thomas; and Thomas obliged him by writing the great *Summa Contra Gentiles.*

Ramon traveled to France and to Rome, everywhere urging that missionaries be prepared by learning the geography, the languages, the customs, and the beliefs of the people to whom they would go. He founded schools for those missionaries. He wrote a religious novel, *Blanquerna*, and beautiful works of mystical devotion, in his native tongue of Catalan. He wrote treatises on logic and on what would come to be called computational theory. He had not the brilliance of Thomas Aquinas, but who has? Yet no one of his time wrote works of such high quality in so wide a range of genres and on so wide a range of subjects. This tireless work occupied him for nearly thirty years.

Then at last Ramon, now a gray-haired man approaching old age, had his chance. The ship was in the sunny harbor of Genoa. Ramon's friends and students had loaded his books on board. Across the sea lay Tunis, a city of some two hundred thousand souls, and the seat of the most powerful Muslim ruler in the west.

But Ramon, sensitive soul that he was, was stricken with terror. It should endear him to us all the more. He could not board the ship. He spent the next night in a sickness of fear and shame, the desire to preach the love of God burning within him, not allowing him a moment's rest. When he heard that another ship was bound for Tunis, Ramon, against the pleadings of his friends, set himself upon it, and at once his heart was filled with peace and joy.

The sea glinted and the waves sloshed against the hull. Only the helmsman Love could steer the way.

Love and reason

So Ramon Llull arrived in the public square of Tunis. "I challenge to prove by reason alone," he cried out, "that the Christian faith is the full truth, and if I am overcome by reason, I vow that I shall myself become a Muslim."

The Arabs took up the challenge. "You are correct," said Ramon, "in your belief that God is almighty and is all-wise. But you have neglected his love and goodness. How can you say that God is preeminent in all things worthy of praise, but when it comes to love and goodness you have nothing to offer but contradictions?"

"Old man," said the imam, not without a man's respect for the brave opponent, "you are walking into the trap that you yourself have set. You grant to us that we are right to uphold the might of God, may his name ever be praised, and yet you believe in an absurdity, that this same Lord should become a man like us, a baby who could not walk, a boy who could not swing a sword, and then the man on the cross, who could not smite his enemies. You pride yourself upon your logic," he continued, glancing at a fascinating device that Ramon had invented, made up of wheels within wheels of propositions leading to inevitable conclusions. "But this is worse than an error in logic. It is blasphemy. Recant, and you shall enjoy the favor of the Sultan."

"It is not error but truth," said Ramon. "Consider. Is it not a mark of the power of God, that he should do what seems unimaginable to us? When the Sultan descends from his litter to assist a beggar in the street, does he not rise in the favor of God, the compassionate, the merciful? Then God showed his power at one with his goodness and his love, when he not only descended from his throne to share our life as one of us, but also submitted to be scorned by us, and scourged by us, and put to death by us. And he rose from the dead, so that we see that his might is his love, and his love is life. For he who loves not, lives not."

The imam left, troubled at heart. This fellow might be dangerous. But when an advisor to the Sultan recommended that the old man be cast into a dungeon and then put to death, he intervened. "My lord," he said, "consider the zeal of the man, and how much we would praise the Muslim who showed such courage." So Ramon Llull was merely banished from the country.

Only love persuades

The sea would beckon again, and in the year 1315, Ramon Llull, a frail man of more than four-score years, was stoned to death by an angry mob of Muslims in the north African city of Bugia. His bones lie in the Church of Saint Francis, in Palma, where he sang of his merry and carnal loves when he was young, and then sang all his life long of the love of God. It is hard to imagine any more promising way than his, to reach the heart of the Muslim. But I will end this essay by letting Llull speak, in one of his most beautiful meditations:

The Lover cried aloud to all men and said, "Love bids you love always—in walking and sitting, waking and sleeping, in speech and in silence, in buying and selling, weeping and laughing, joy and sorrow, gain and loss. In whatever you do, you must love, for this is Love's commandment."

℘ ℘ ℘

MOTHER OF UNIVERSITIES

⁕

Eystein leaned over the side of the ship, his flax-light hair tousled in the breeze. He was steady on his feet as the waves rolled, a true lad of Norway, at home on the water. Eystein had often rowed from his father's farm at the head of the fjord, down to the busy town of Nidaros, the seat of the archbishop. Now he could see the single spire of Saint Olav's Church receding in the distance, and it wrung his heart with love. "Eystein," said the bishop, "when you go to Paris, our Nidaros will seem little more than a summer hamlet for hunters and shepherds." Eystein had no idea how that could be true.

So here he was, aboard a ship bound for France. He carried a letter of introduction to the prior of one of the most famous schools in the world, at the Abbey Saint-Victor. Eystein spoke no French. That was all right, though. The late prior of Saint-Victor, the brilliant philosopher Hugh, was a Saxon. Eystein had heard tell of a mystical theologian there named Richard, from Scotland. Eystein would meet young men from all over Christendom. They spoke Latin, the language of the Church. Sure, there would be rivalry among the nationals, and much drink, and snow-ball fights, and nodding off at the bench during lectures. But imagine, wise and learned men from Italy, France, Germany, England, Spain, and now farthest Norway, united there to take into their minds and hearts the Word of God, the order and beauty of his creation, and the laws of human thought and action. "Lord," said Eystein, "help me to bring your wisdom back to my beloved land."

When Eystein finally rode into Paris, he thought the world had never seen anything like it—and he was right. Yet the first stone for the magnificent Cathedral of Notre Dame had yet to be laid, and the pupils and masters of Saint-Victor, Saint-Genevieve, and Notre Dame had not yet formed the *universitas scholarium*: the union or guild of scholars, come together to secure their liberties, and to assure that awards of degrees would depend upon knowledge, not upon where you came from or what money you had. Yes, the *university* was a Medieval guild, born from the bosom of the Church. And *colleges*? Dormitories for students, to keep them out of trouble!

Never before

If Eystein had been born in Italy at the time of Cicero, and if his father had had the money, he'd have gone to a school for boys, and then, as a young man, he might have traveled overseas to Athens, to study at the old Academy founded by Plato. Other philosophers too had founded academies; so why don't we call them universities?

There was no set course of study, acknowledged as valid everywhere. Masters did not come from everywhere to unite in the pursuit of truth, and to pass their knowledge to their successors, granting them the license to teach for other scholarly guilds: at Oxford, Bologna, Prague, Coimbra, Valencia, Kraków. There was no universally recognized degree: bachelor, doctor, master. Most of all, there was no common faith, no common worship of God, no theology of the revealed Word of God—theology, the queen of the sciences, the one field of study uniting in itself the truths from all the other fields.

What was developing at Paris when Eystein Erlendsson studied there would become a happy coincidence of two meanings of the Latin *universitas*. It would be a union bound by union: by a common faith in the God who made the universe, in whom we live and move and have our being.

And because we're talking about the Church, we are also in the realm of the universal society founded by Christ upon earth. The Church was the first World Wide Web, caring for her children wherever they lived, and sending her priests to teach kings and peasants, farmers and townsmen, merchants and wheelwrights—everyone. Eystein knew it well. Saint Olav, King of Norway, had begged the Church to send missionaries to his land, to tame the ways of his warlike country-men, and bring them the light of Christ. It was Olav who had made Nidaros a northern aurora of Christian life.

An examination for all to behold

It's a few years later, and we see Eystein stand-ing before the teachers of Saint-Victor, in the open air. The teachers are robed in their clerical garb. Grocer girls mill about, selling hot loaves from baskets. The owner of an inn across the way stands in his garden, beckoning people to come in and refresh themselves. Some schoolboys climb a beech tree to get a better view. Just as you can't have a real celebration unless heaven and earth are invited, so here, in Paris, as will be the case for a long time after, you can't have a real examination unless everyone can behold it. For the questions bear upon everyone and everything, even now, long before Thomas Aquinas, from southern Italy by way of Cologne, will teach in Paris and write his all-comprehending *Summa Theologiae*.

"Augustinus," says the master, "if a king should demand something that does not violate the natural law, but does violate the liberty of the Church to correct and punish her own, is he to be obeyed? Saint Paul says that all authority is of God, and the Lord Christ says we must render to Caesar what is his."

The boys in the tree lean forward—this is a *live question*. They're used to odd-looking people from strange places, but the tall and fair Eystein holds their attention.

The masters don't want Eystein's opinion. What good is that? Nor a flash of rhetorical fire. They want reason, they want the Word of God. They want truth.

"Master," says Eystein, furrowing his brow, "we must draw distinctions. Authority derives not from the king's will, but from the nature and scope of the office which God has conferred upon him." With a clear voice and bright eyes, Eystein enumerates those things that a king *may not do*, because even a king is subject to the law of God, wherever he may be king. A woman in the crowd, the daughter of a duke, listens intently. This truth is for everyone. A young Englishman named Thomas, Eystein's good friend, smiles with approval, even as he leans the woman's way—for Thomas is young, and his heart has not yet been pierced by holy love.

One saint to another

"My dear Thomas," writes Eystein—if you'll allow me the liberty of imagining the gist of letters he wrote to his old friend, now Archbishop of Canterbury—"I applaud you in your course of action. You must know that we are engaged in the same battle. It is always the same. Here the Duke Sverre has set himself against good King Magnus, and he has won a few priests to his side, though I fear that if he should ascend the throne of Norway, those priests would soon learn what beast they had thought to tame. Then must the Church be compelled to duck and kiss the feet of the king, and take her orders from him rather than from God. The people will learn how careful and merciful a mother the Church is, when they have instead to treat with ambitious and unscrupulous men."

King Henry II of England wanted to subject priests to the civil courts, rather than the ecclesiastical courts, and he expected that Thomas, the playfellow of his youth and his former chancellor, would use that great learning of his to support the cause. But Thomas proved to be God's soldier first, fighting the encroachments of the court and the arbitrary taxes that Henry tried to levy. Then followed many years of struggle. The king by no means had his way, for the common people were not with him. In those days, even the king knew he was a king only by the grace of God. Henry and Thomas and Eystein dwelt in the same universe of meaning.

So one day, in exasperation, Henry cried, "Will no man rid me of this pestilent priest?" Some courtiers took him at his word; and Saint Eystein's friend Thomas was murdered in Canterbury Cathedral, on December 29, 1170, while he was at vespers. Eystein later went to England himself, bringing back to Norway inspiration for the cathedral he would build at Nidaros—modern Trondheim—and the veneration of the holy martyr Thomas Becket.

The name remains

That is a glimpse of the world of the first universities. The grandest building in Paris was not a box for bureaucrats, or a glass tower of moneymaking. It was a church; and she gathered her own to her haven, from every land and clime. What was the University of Paris? It and not the royal court was the heart of the most fruitful city in the world. Let Saint Louis IX of France testify. From Paris, wrote the king, "flow the most abundant waters of wholesome doctrine, so that they become a great river which after refreshing the city itself irrigates the Universal Church."

In 1793, the French revolutionaries, flush with the cruelty of the secular idea, shut the University of Paris down. It remained shut for a hundred years.

The western world still has what we call universities, but they bear little resemblance to their long-gone grandparents. Degrees remain, and academic regalia, and the residue of an expected course of study. Whether they bring forth wise men and women, even saints and martyrs, is another question. Catholic universities ought to ask it.

ℭℭ ℭℭ ℭℭ

EUROPE SET FREE

‧⁕⁙⁖⁕‧

The young priest quietly opened the door to the private chambers of his superior. He was holding a tray with some bread and cheese and wine. Before him, kneeling on the floor, was an old man in a white robe. His head was bowed, and his lean countenance bore the furrows of long habits of severe self-discipline. In his hands was a black rosary. His fingers moved from one bead to the next.

"Holy Father," said the priest, "I have brought you some refreshment."

A slight nod from the old man was the only reply. The priest set the tray on a table and left the chambers, shutting the door. In the halls he met one of his fellow servants. "On his knees," was all he said. The old man had been on his knees all night.

From an open window came the fresh breeze of the fall, a sunny, musty scent of hayricks and ripening fruit. A man with a cart full of apples trundled down the street, calling out his wares. Children played a noisy game with a ball. Women came back from the baker's with baskets of loaves, balancing them on their heads with one hand, the

76

other hand free for Italian conversation. All over the city near the sea, and in a hundred seaport cities all over Europe, there were these sights and sounds and smells; but in Rome that old man knelt and prayed, because on his shoulders lay the burden of this decisive morning, October 7, 1571.

Then he rose and joined the cardinals in consistory. Work to be done.

De profundis

Sometimes, once a week when João smiled, you could see that he had been a beautiful youth, with glossy dark hair and high cheekbones, but in a moment that hint of beauty would harden into settled hopelessness and hatred, like a mask. He was a merchant's son from Oporto, and had had the rounded muscles of a young man used to loading and unloading ships, with their barrels of wine and oil and casks of spices, muscles softened by the sleek flesh you get when you eat well and drink well. Now all that was left of him was bone and sinew, and the mask. Most of his hair had fallen out. His skin was taut and yellow, with hardly a shred to hide his nakedness. The stench of human excretion round about him was abominable. Lice nested in his hair and crawled upon his flesh, but he had ceased to care. His feet were in irons and his hands dared not let go of the oar.

A turbaned Turk with a whip lashed about him left and right, crying, "Pull, pull!" In the hull of that galley were two hundred prisoners, many of them Christians seized by Turkish raiders from ships at sea or from the ports exposed to their piracy. João was one of those galley slaves. He'd once hoped to be sold back for ransom, but the hope had passed. All he knew of the outside world was what he managed to pick up from the scattered Turkish he had learned in the past two years. He would die in this stinking hull. There was no question of that. But he prayed that his tormentors would sink to the bottom of the sea with him. For this morning they were going into battle.

He had no idea what day it was. He had no idea what month it was, though it seemed, from the little he could glimpse through the oar-holes, that the days were growing shorter.

"Break their teeth in their mouths, O Lord," he prayed, "break the teeth of the lions!"

A more pleasant meeting

It's the same day, in Vienna. A small congregation of men have gathered in the cellarage of a local nobleman whose protection they enjoy.

Farther down the Danube River, the Turks are well established, so that Vienna has long been a city under siege. Its people have been riven with dissent; some are Catholic, some favor Luther, some favor Calvin, and some, like the men in the cellarage, look upon all of the others alike as dreadful heretics. These men are called by their enemies *Anabaptists*, meaning people who baptize themselves all over again, considering the baptism in infancy to be of no effect.

"Don John and the fleets from Genoa and Venice set sail ten days ago," says their leader. Don John is the brother of the Hapsburg king of Austria, Maximilian.

"Then the League of Evil meets the infidel upon the high sea," he continues. "If the League should be victorious, then the Turks will be hungry for vengeance. We should then expect the Danube to run red with Austrian blood. That may well be to our purpose. We shall be masters then, since the Turk will never be able to hold the city without our assistance. If the Turks are victorious, then Don John is put to shame and the Archpriest of Satan is foiled."

"Either way," says one of his fellows, "there is something to seek, and something to fear."

"Let us then pray that the will of God be done."

They are not thinking of men such as João, but then, Vienna is not a town on the seacoast.

Queen and devoted subject

The royal court in Windsor. A woman with red hair, something too pointed of a nose, shrewd active eyes, and restless hands looks at the young seaman before her.

"So," she says, "you have been peppering Spanish ships in the Indies, have you?"

"Yes, my liege."

"Yet you return to my court with holes in your shoes and a hat that a bargeman would be ashamed to wear."

"We must both give and take in battle, my liege." But he was smoldering.

"You should be more careful than to measure your might in battle with my brother of Spain," said the queen, with a wry grin. The king of Spain, Philip II, was the husband of her none-too-beloved sister Mary, who now lay moldering in her tomb.

"I shall be to them like a fiery thorn," he replied. "If you will help me to rig a ship. Your majesty, only a few thousand pounds"—but she stopped him. She squeezed the pommels of her throne as a man might squeeze an orange.

"I do not finance pirates," she said. "But if you should like a ship to bring me *news* and *commodities* from distant islands and coastlands," she said, wryly, "I shall not take it amiss. I cannot afford anything lavish, you understand."

"Perfectly, your majesty."

Then she twisted her form upon the throne as her mind returned to a preoccupation. "You have been defeated by Spaniards," she said, with some scorn.

"As I said, my queen, we gave and we took."

"The Holy League, we hear, will set upon the Turk in the Greek seas. Perhaps they are even now at it. What think you?" She seemed to be asking a sailor about naval warfare, but in her mind's eye she saw an old crabbed man penning the writ that excommunicated her from the Church, her, a throned monarch! Yet she knew that England was stuffed full of cousins with royal blood. The pestilent Cardinal Pole himself had been one of them. Indeed, her firmest *legal* claim to the throne was that she happened to be sitting upon it.

"No cause for worry," he said. "The Turks are unmatched on the water."

"God's blood!" she spluttered. "You take much upon you! You think I wish the death of Christians at the hands of infidels?" But she calmed down and motioned him to come forward, extending her hand to kiss.

"Master Drake," she said, "you shall have your ship."

You teach my fingers to fight

We are on board the royal ship of the Christian fleet, off the port of Lepanto, on October 7, 1571. The pope had ordered that all the men aboard should be shriven before battle, and should pray the rosary. Strict discipline must be maintained. No coarse or blasphemous language; no grumbling; no excess of meat or drink. Don John was meeting with the other chiefs. What should they do? The weather was poor, and they appeared to be outnumbered, and the Turk had long been master of the sea. Many of the chiefs recommended delay, to wait for a more propitious time.

"My lord," said one of the admirals, "I am not a learned man, nor can I tell the future, but Peter has commanded the attack, and I will put my trust in him!"

"So be it then!" said Don John. "We will attack!"

And they did. Far away in Rome, the old man suddenly rose from among the cardinals, looked out the window, and cried, "Enough of business! We must now thank God for the victory he has given the Christian army!"

The Battle of Lepanto marked the beginning of the end of Turkish dominance in the Mediterranean, setting the ports free of the terror from the east. Thousands of galley slaves like João were liberated. A young Spanish nobleman whom we know well as Cervantes fought valiantly in the battle and lost the use of one hand; he was ever after to boast that it was the greatest thing he had ever done in his life. The Poles would, time and again, drive the Turks back down the

Danube, saving Europe from the east. Merchants in the north of Europe could ply their trades because Spanish, Italian, Austrian, and Polish soldiers made it possible. They saved the continent for freedom.

When confirmation of the victory reached Rome, the city erupted into joyous celebration. A new feast day was declared: the Feast of the Holy Rosary.

The old man in Rome died the next year. We call him Saint Pius V.

එ එ එ

THERE WAS A SOLDIER
SENT FROM GOD

·ᵉᵒᵥᴥᴥᵍᵥ·

"John," said the captain, "you're a fine soldier, and a young man of courage and honor. If
you join our cause, I guarantee you an officer's
commission." The cause was just, as Captain
Magruder saw it. They would be fighting to protect a venerable confederation of states from invasion by a hostile power. It was March 1863, and
Fort Sumter had been fired upon and seized by
the men of South Carolina. The government in
Washington would not stand for it. Invasion was
inevitable.

The youth was twenty years old, tall and
clean-shaven. He spoke English with a strange accent. His father had been executed by ministers
of the Russian tsar for having taken part in a desperate attempt to free his native Poland from her
grip. For Poland had been carved up for the ambitious monarchs of eastern Europe to dine upon,
most notably the able and ravenous Frederick
the Great of Prussia, and the equally able and
depraved Catherine the Great of Russia. Such is
greatness in this world.

The boy and his mother were permitted to
visit him the day before the execution. He had

84

been mewed up in a filthy hole for thirteen months, without once being allowed to wash or to change his clothing. The father wept and blessed them, and they parted, mother and son to leave their native land and their ancestral home forever. She died soon after, and the boy made his way to America.

"Captain Magruder," said the youth, "I came here as an exile, without home or country. The United States has given me both. I will always be true to the government of my adoption. I will fight behind its flag, and if it should go down to defeat or disaster, I will go with it."

The men parted as friends. The youth was true to his words. He fought at some of the bloodiest battles the world had seen: Bull Run, Chancellorsville, Antietam, and Gettysburg. He was shot through the stomach and astonished the doctors by surviving—to rejoin the Union army. He remembered little of the Catholic faith of his boyhood, and he never returned to it, though he later became a national leader of Christian pro-gressives, fighting for woman suffrage and against the liquor trade. His name was John Sobieski, the last survivor of the greatest royal line of Poland, a shadow, though a noble shadow, of the man who saved Europe from destruction.

The watchman on the tower

September 12, 1683. A sentinel climbs wearily to his post, overlooking the broad valley of the Danube, whose divided waters surround his city, Vienna. Her people are suffering from hunger and disease. They have been huddling within her walls for several months, while all about her swarm the armies of the Turkish sultan, six hundred thousand men, with their barbarous songs, their camels and elephants, and their battering rams that have already made breaches in the walls. The people have been waiting for help from Germany, help from France, help from any of the other European powers. Nothing. Their king and court have fled. The commander of the city has announced that if their last hope, Poland, does not come to rescue them, they will yield to the Turks. This is the date he has set for surrender.

And on this morning, the feast of the Holy Name of Mary, the sentinel sees something new in the distance—men on horseback, and the dragon-banners of the Polish king! It's a small army, no more than one man for every six of the Turks. But one Polish warrior was worth far more than that. "He is here, John Sobieski is here," he cries, and the defenders of the city take up arms again, and the women rejoice and flock to the churches to pray.

John Sobieski had broken the teeth of the Turks at the battle of Choczim, twelve years before. His name was a tower of strength. Even so, the Germans in his army rose in mutiny. Why should they hurl themselves into the maw of so numerous an enemy?

So Sobieski the king rose to speak.

"We are to fight a battle today, not for spoliation and plunder, but for the cross. While we contend with an army apparently so overwhelming in numbers, yet encamped around, about, and above us are the invisible hosts of heaven, who will bring confusion to the foe and victory to our arms. This day, by the blessing of Almighty God and the Christian's Christ and Redeemer, we are to crush yonder exultant foe, and write such a page in the world's history that will cause mankind to glorify the cross in all ages to come."

Down upon the overweening and careless Turkish army swept the cavalry of this good and brave man, King John III Sobieski. There was an eclipse of the sun that day, and to the superstitious Turks it was as if the Polish king blazed out in glory against the darkness. The sultan's force was demolished. Turkish armies would never again threaten western Europe; and if there are now many thousands of people speaking Arabic in the streets of Paris, that is not the fault of John Sobieski.

The Archbishop of Vienna met the king on the next morning, and before the joyful crowds he declared, "There was a man sent from God, whose name was John."

No good deed goes unpunished

The king summed up his campaign by piously revising Caesar's boast: *Veni, vidi, Deus vicit—I came, I saw; God conquered.*

That was no empty piety, no political posturing for the masses. John Sobieski had no lust for empire. He gave Europe back to Europe, and Austria back to Austria.

So how did the crowned heads of Europe repay the Poles who had saved them from the tidal wave of the Turks?

It's hard for us to imagine, but when the king's sixth great-grandson John was fighting for the Union in the Civil War, Poland was for many people as vague and fabulous as Atlantis. The colonel said he met a woman who thought that it was somewhere in China. Others thought, with good reason, that it was somewhere in Russia.

At the Congress of Vienna in 1815, after the defeat of Napoleon, in whose armies against the Russians many Polish soldiers fought, the partition was sealed for a century. England and the nations of western Europe forgot that for two hundred years their liberties were secured against

Turkish invastions by the Poles. They sold out the partitioners, with Russia getting the lion's share and calling it a Polish "kingdom," though it was ruled by the tsar's ministers, who tried to obliterate Polish culture.

Some still remember

Meanwhile, one faraway nation, not yet a world power, did value the Polish fight for liberty. One month after the signing of the Declaration of Independence, a young Polish man newly arrived in Philadelphia offered his services to the Continental Army. His name was Tadeusz Kościuszko—a name well known to schoolchildren in the days when Americans still revered their forefathers. He was an engineer, and George Washington asked him to build a fortress at some strategic point along the Hudson River. Kościuszko chose a site called West Point.

He was a great hero of the Revolutionary War, but his accomplishments upon the battlefield were exceeded by what he later accomplished by means of his friendship with Thomas Jefferson. He had been trained in a military school in France, and so he naturally urged his beloved Americans to establish a similar school for the training of officers. They finally did so—at West Point. When a grateful Congress raised him to the rank of brigadier general, with back pay, Kosciuszko set the money aside to be given at his death for the emancipation of slaves and their training. Jefferson was named the executor of his will.

Salvation from the forgotten land

Kościuszko returned to Poland in 1794, to fight the powers threatening to partition his native land. In this attempt he was thwarted by temporizing noblemen, who persuaded the Polish government to appeal to the heads of Europe, rather than to entrust themselves to Kościuszko's initial military victory. They lost their freedom for a hundred years. Kościuszko's remains lie in the royal Wawel Castle, where, among many other Polish kings, John III Sobieski had ruled.

Nations do not normally rise from the ashes. Frederick's Prussia died, and will never be seen again. Poland died, but she rose again. Or rather Poland never died, because Poland was more than a geographical area or a form of government or a style of music or cookery or whatever else we now call culture. Poland was Catholic. Poland had the Faith.

When Henryk Sienkiewicz came to visit America in 1876, the centenary of our independence, he had not yet written *With Fire and Sword*, his trilogy of novels about the battles of the Poles against the Turks. He had not yet written *Quo Vadis?*, his epic about the first Christians and their testament of faith in the face of Roman persecution. But consider that in him, as in the Poles generally, lay hidden that ardent love of liberty which was a love for their homeland, and a love for God and his Church.

The Poles loved America, when America loved true liberty, and that brings us to another Polish warrior, who honored John Sobieski and Tadeusz Kościuszko, who treasured Sienkiewicz, and who had suffered under the yoke of a now-godless Russia. He would have had opportunity, as a youth, to visit the tombs of Sobieski and Kościuszko, because Wawel Castle is in Kraków, where this athletic and passionate young man would one day rule as archbishop.

He too visited America, as Pope John Paul II, filling Yankee Stadium with cheering crowds. He called upon Americans to remember what it is to be a nation under God, and to remember that true liberty is inseparable from virtue. In a few short years, the back of the Russian bear—considered indomitable by know-it-alls of our time—would be broken, and Poland would be free again, thanks in large part to this soldier in the white robes.

Whether America will be free remains to be seen. For John Paul II came not to beg aid from us, but to offer himself for us, as King John had done long ago for the Christian world.

THE PLAYWRIGHT
THE PROFESSORS HAVE
REJECTED

◦⟡◦

It's Saint Stephen's Day, the day after Christmas, 1604. We are in Windsor Castle, in a palatial room decked for the season in holly and ivy. Aromas of rich food and drink fill the air. Hundreds of lords and ladies are there, but they are silent, all eyes and ears fixed upon what is happening before them. Even King James leans forward from his seat of honor, elevated above the rest.

A man in the garb of a friar, no friar but the Duke of Vienna, is pronouncing sentence upon his deputy Angelo, who is by intention guilty of raping a young nun as blackmail for sparing her brother's life, and then having the brother executed anyway. The brother's crime was not rape or blackmail or murder, but merely getting his own betrothed wife with child. Angelo richly deserves to die, and wishes it. But he, too, is loved. His own betrothed wife, Mariana, whom he has spurned, pleads for him. The nun, Isabella, believing that her brother is dead, stands in the midst as accuser and victim.

The Duke speaks with all the authority of natural justice, law, and Holy Writ:

> *But as he adjudged your brother—*
> *Being criminal, in double violation*
> *Of sacred chastity and promise-breach*
> *Thereon dependent, for your brother's life,—*

and the great actor Richard Burbage raises his right arm to the heavens,

> *The very mercy of the law cries out*
> *Most audible, even from his proper tongue,*
> *An Angelo for Claudio, death for death.*
> *Haste still pays haste, and leisure answers leisure;*
> *Like doth quit like, and Measure still for Measure.*

One of the actors, a middle-aged man in the small part of a friar, looks on. He nods. "Dick's a genius," he thinks. "Not one word overdone. Brilliant, my old friend!" The friar is the leader of the theatrical company, The King's Men. He's also the author and director of the play.

The people in the audience are taken off guard. Just for a moment, they look into their hearts, as the author hoped they would. They know the words of Jesus: *Judge not, that you may not be judged. For with what judgment you judge, you shall be judged: and with what measure you mete, it shall be measured to you again.* They know that Angelo is a villain. But what man alive can hold his head high before his Savior? They are not sentimentalists. No one in that room is; certainly not the author. It is the day after Christmas. What will happen?

Mariana turns to Isabella, one woman to another. "Isabel," she cries, "sweet Isabel, do yet but kneel by me!" She begs the nun to plead for the life of the man who would have raped her, and who, as everyone believes, has enacted a judicial murder of her brother. What will happen? Souls hang in the balance.

The director counts to himself, one, two, three, four.… Not yet, Nicky, not yet, lad…now! Isabella falls to her knees.

The king and the king's man

After the festivities, the king, sober and thoughtful, calls the director over. "Master William, you are worth a thousand parsons."

"I am no parson, my liege," says William. "Several tapsters on the Thames could testify to that. You know that our jests are unfit for any holy place."

The king narrows his eyes with a good-natured but ironical glare. "Is it fit for you to bandy words with your sovereign? A thousand parsons, I say."

"I humbly thank your majesty."

The king prides himself on being something of a theologian, as William knows. "I refer to the text upon which your play has been so splendid a commentary."

"*Measure for Measure*," says William.

"No," says the king. "You see, I too am aware of the times and the seasons." And he reads from the psalm for Christmas day:

> *Mercy and justice have met each other:*
> > *justice and peace have kissed.*
> *Truth is sprung out of the earth:*
> > *and justice hath looked down from heaven.*

"As I had expected," says William. "My king is attentive and wise."

"Now, your Isabella pleads for the life of her persecutor. There is mercy. But she pleads on the grounds that Angelo did not perform the rape he believed he performed, and that he did have warrant *by the letter of the law* to execute her brother. There is law, there is justice." The king pauses. "Explain yourself."

"My liege," says William, "you need no wisdom from me, but I will obey. Our Savior put the old law to death by fulfilling its terms to the letter, raising it to life in the spirit, in the new law of mercy. For mercy and justice in this world seldom speak to one another, but in heaven they are sisters, and they kiss."

"Which is why you have given me this Christmas gift," says King James of England.

"I am honored to do so," says Shakespeare.

Playwright of feasts

I've heard people say, dismissively, that Charles Dickens "invented" Christmas for the English. That's nonsense. The grog and ale had long been there, the gift-giving, the caroling, and the witness of the Gospels, telling how Love came down among us in the flesh. English writers have been meditating upon the two most dramatic feasts of the faith, Christmas and Easter, ever since the monks made the Saxons literate and Christian.

Shakespeare was no exception. When James ascended the throne in 1603, Shakespeare was already a writer of renown, head and shoulders above his theatrical fellows. But in that age of theological ferment—when collections of sermons could make good money for booksellers—Shakespeare was also, by far, the most theological of his fellows. It isn't that he simply echoes Scripture more often than they do. It's that some of his plays, like *Measure for Measure*, are inspired by theological reflection and are organized accordingly.

The favor that his company received from James meant he would present plays before the court during other Christmas holidays. That alone would have sufficed to encourage him to meditate upon the meaning of Christmas, and to portray that meaning in unusual dramatic form. Yet Shakespeare, of all people, could not easily avoid thinking about the specifics of his faith. He was a Roman Catholic living in a realm that persecuted Roman Catholics. His father had died a recusant. His daughter Susanna would also be openly Roman. His cousin, Robert Southwell, was a poet and a Jesuit priest, executed by Queen Elizabeth.

Take Christmas and Easter, and Shakespeare's final three plays. *Cymbeline* is set during the reign of the king who ruled England when Christ was born. The universal peace fit for the Prince of Peace is secured in England by a truce between Cymbeline and the Roman army. The play's repentant hero is named Postumus, for his having been born after his father had died. He is, morally and dramatically, raised from the dead; as is his innocent wife Imogen. *The Winter's Tale* involves a royal newborn baby, abandoned to the elements, discovered by illiterate shepherds. It too features a resurrection from the dead—in the most startling final scene of any that has ever graced the stage.

The Tempest was inspired by a wondrous account of men lost at sea. They had been shipwrecked off Bermuda, but they survived, and the news reached England a year later, in December 1608. It was the talk of the town. Meditating upon that, and upon the daily readings for Advent and Christmastide, Shakespeare wrote his farewell to the stage. *The Tempest* is filled with mysterious echoes of the prophet Isaiah, of the shipwreck of Saint Paul, and of the birth of Jesus. A small child is exposed to death by evil and envious men, but is miraculously saved; and a man dead in sin, believed by his son to be drowned, is raised up, undergoing "a sea change/ Into something rich and strange." In all of these last plays, salvation comes from the small, the child, the stone which the builders rejected. Out of the mouths of babes, indeed.

Pearls of great price

So how do we teach the works of the greatest author who ever lived?

Imagine going to Chartres Cathedral, to study how much the granite cost, and to inspect the water table under the foundation, but not gazing up at the rose windows in their glory.

Imagine going to the Sistine Chapel, taking a tape measure to Michelangelo's Adam, to record the length and width of arm and neck and big toe, but not looking in awe at the longing in his countenance, and his finger waiting for the electric touch of God.

Imagine being at Bethany, and asking Lazarus (once the shrouds were off) what he thought of

Roman politics. Imagine being near Solomon's Portico at Pentecost, and inquiring about what dialect of Cretan the Cretans heard the Apostles preaching in. Imagine being there when Jesus healed the blind man, and asking him about his corns.

It might be better never to have been in those places than to have been there as someone worse than deaf and blind. Yet the riches remain, for those with the heart to open the treasure chest and look.

℘ ℘ ℘

Beloved Physician
and Teller of Truth

※◦◦◦◇◇◯◦◦◦※

In the days before the telephone, people wrote letters to one another, and that included little boys sent to boarding school. One such lad named Horatio wrote his first letter home from Cape Cod, with this *p.s.*: "I have just come home from the seashore and as I have leisure I will add a few words. I like the school and the scholars very much. I go to the Quaker meeting. I have not been homesick in the least since I came down." Typical boy.

Horatio Storer was eight when he wrote that. He loved the seashore and its life: fish, seals, mollusks, seaweed. So after he was through with his Latin, he wandered on the beach or set out on the water. "Last Friday," he writes, at age nine, "the boys went down to Scorten Harbor and stayed all day. We made a great fire out of logs and dried beach grass, and we roasted some menhaden which we had got while the men were seining shad." His letters are filled with adventures; walking six miles to see the skeleton of a white shark, combing the woods to collect birds' eggs; hewing logs with other boys for a cabin complete with

American flags and a portrait of "Tippecanoe" Harrison; and, when he was a Harvard lad, sailing all the way to Labrador.

Horatio grew up strong, immensely curious, keenly observant, and a student of God's creatures in all their wondrous forms. The Storers were Quakers, but Horatio was an explorer in faith too, as his future would show.

Horatio Storer, M.D.

Horatio's parents wanted him to be a doctor. When he was a boy he thought that studying medicine would be drudgery. But from the start Horatio was fascinated by life: what made plants and animals what they were. As a teenager he sailed to Nova Scotia with a naturalist searching for embryos of birds and fish to examine them under a microscope: they were at the beginning of embryology. They put ashore once and went to Methodist services, Horatio noting that the attendance put Boston to shame. He cared about that.

An 1850 letter to the *Boston Journal* shows his interest in public questions. Racialist theories were in the air. Apologists for slavery sought scientific approval. They looked for evidence that the human race *was not one*. So when a freak of nature—a dwarf sheep—appeared in England, and the owner then allegedly bred a flock of them, racialists claimed that something like that had happened among isolated human populations, producing different species. Young Storer would have nothing of it. He cast the whole story in doubt, seeing where the leap of reasoning tended, and insisting, as a scientist, that evidence for racialist claims was utterly lacking.

In short, Horatio Storer, M.D., was not just a genial doctor whose hands had been trained to heal. He was a scientist and man of prayer, in love with truth and the glory of God's creation. It's no surprise when we find him, at age twenty-six, writing a letter that proved momentous in American history. Dr. Storer had treated several women with bad complications after an abortion. He could not remain silent. "I am just now working up certain statistics on the subject of criminal abortion. If you can put me in the way of ascertaining the proportionate number of still births of last year or for a series of years in any of our large American cities…I shall be greatly obliged."

The Facts of the Case

Storer faced a moral conundrum. Doctors had been looking the other way when it came to *all gynecological issues*. Horatio Storer established the nation's *first hospital ward for gynecology*.

So too it was with abortion. The doctors were not sensitive so much as timid; not moral but self-protecting. But Storer would not let them evade the issue. Intentional abortion, he argued, is necessarily "occasioned by the 'malice afore-thought' of the law."

Medicine was not then a political nerve-center. Storer had to demonstrate a medical fact. The moral and political consequences would follow. If it can be determined that there is a living human being inside a hut, and I burn the hut down, I am guilty *in fact* of homicide. Well then, embryology had progressed far enough for Storer, with his keen powers of observation and logical deduction, to show that a child in the womb is its own "nervous center, self-existing, self-acting," not inert, like an acorn, or a parasite, like a tapeworm.

Think of the time between conception and implantation, when the fertilized cell travels from the ovary to the womb. That time proves, said Storer, that the embryo is *independent*. But it is irrational to suppose that it is so for a day or two, and then is merged back into the *identity* of the mother. Therefore it is impossible to hold that human life "dates from any other epoch than conception." The leading doctors of the time agreed, and laws were reformed accordingly.

Words and Deeds

His deeds paint a fuller picture. He earned a law degree at Harvard to assist lawyers in fighting the good fight; that was at his own expense. Yet he was merciful to troubled women. He admitted unwed mothers—they had nowhere else to go—to the "lying-in" hospital where he worked in Boston, to help them as best he could, and counsel them against taking wrong decisions.

Those who know they need God's grace are apt to forgive others too. At age thirty-nine, the one-time sailor boy wrote these words: "Compelled humbly to surrender to the Master my life had denied, I find a peace of which before I had had no conception, and then strangely enough, the harbor of refuge for which my ships at sea had been so long and so ineffectually struggling was reached at last on Christmas Eve." He had accepted the Trinity.

Horatio Storer, Catholic

That, however, was not the end of the voyage, for in his fifties Horatio Storer became a Roman Catholic. Imagine—a Harvard graduate, living in New England among Irish immigrants and the native English who detested them. But truth leads where it leads, and you follow it because you must. He settled in Newport, and became one of the most beloved citizens of Rhode Island. He was the last surviving member of his graduating class, retaining his sharp mind and his devout heart till his death in 1922, at age ninety-two.

He loved the Church, humbly taking instruction from her just as he had taken instruction from the men of science when he was a boy. He had to stand up for victims of racial bigotry again: French immigrants, even nuns, whom the Irish and other native Rhode Islanders didn't want around. Storer begged his friend the bishop to intervene, and he prevailed.

In his letter to the bishop we find words that would honor any Catholic in any state of life: "It is my constant prayer that if ever our Lord should permit me to do some slight thing for him, and should say to me as to Saint Thomas of Aquinas [that I had spoken well of him and might receive what I would], grace might be given me to answer, *Domine, non nisi Te.* Nothing, Lord, but Thee."

ʕ⊃ ʕ⊃ ʕ⊃

THE RISING OF THE VENDÉE

Jacques was hardly more than a boy, with a shock of black hair curling about his forehead. Plenty of men in France these days called themselves "Jacques" and rose up against the gentry, seizing their lands and sometimes their throats, while the national barber did its clean work in the *Place de la Concorde* in Paris, and blood ran like wash. But this boy was really named after Saint James. And now he sat in a barge with a hundred other men and boys, as the craft floated down the sluggish Loire, westward towards the sea and the dying day.

The sun glowered through the smoke like the eye of a beast. There was smoke all round, and the glare of fires far off. It was cold and bitter. Père Francois the curé paused in his prayer to look over his shoulder. Then he turned to pray again.

This was the work of Robespierre and his men of light. They profaned the Cathedral of Our Lady in Paris, parading a whore in place of the Mother of God and calling her the goddess Reason. They seized Church lands "for the republic" and put them up for sale. They made the clergy swear to be state puppets, their electors to include any drunken ruffians or atheists who lived in the parish. If the priests did not swear, there was the barber. They suppressed the monastic life, the birthplace of so many holy works and prayers. They dared to alter the time of God, depriving men of their Sabbath rest, replacing it with the rationalist's *decadi*, every tenth day, for the exhibition of patriotic sentiment, or else. They stripped religion bare, inventing for social utility the worship of *L'Être Suprême*, who was neither Father nor Son nor Holy Spirit.

They sent nuns to the scaffold, their only offense that they would not offend. They laid hands on the kindly King Louis himself and his innocent wife and children. Their enlightened hatred knew no bounds.

"I see what Parisians mean by *fraternité*," said Jacques. The soldiers from Mainz who stormed his village were not bellowing in French. Assassins for pay: only from the throats of assassins could come sounds so ugly. They and the republican army put the Vendée to the torch, slaughtering every man they could reach, not sparing women and children. The marshes of the lower Loire, rich in pitch-pines, thick with the peaty soil where you could just toss a seed and it would grow—the plains that Jacques and his family had drained and plowed for three hundred years were laid waste, with a stench of burnt swamp grass and turpentine and bitumen and death. It was Frenchmen murdering their brothers in the name of the brotherhood of man. It looked like the end of the world.

"Why has this happened, Monsieur le Curé?" said Jacques.

"For the same reason it always happens," said the curé. "Men have forgotten God." And the Loire seeped through the cracks of the barge and rose up over their shoes.

Pass the pamphlet

The modern myth of the benign revolution is hard to shake. The most powerful nation on earth, the United States, won her freedom by a war that historians call Revolutionary; though the colonists thought of it as a war for political independence from the mother country, securing the rights of Englishmen under common law. Most of America's founders were wary of revolution, and were in that way more Roman and republican than the self-styled republicans of France. When you assassinate Caesar, you do not get a mild Brutus instead. You get libertine Antony and cold-hearted Octavian and their lists of men to be assassinated, with Octavian giving up Cicero to Antony, and Antony giving up his own brother to Octavian. When you send the meek Louis XVI to the guillotine, you do not get the prissy

Voltaire instead. You get Marat and Saint-Just and Robespierre and the Reign of Terror.

Modern revolutions have never really come from the common people. The landsmen of the Vendée did not hate their masters. Something about working in the earth breeds a hardy race of men who hold their heads high, even as they doff their hats to greet the marquis when he reviews the fields. Pamphlets don't unite. Mud unites. Revolutionary slogans don't stick to such men. Clay sticks. And when the lord dismounts and you walk with him into the marshes, your rifle slung over the shoulder, slogging on to the covert in the cold before daybreak, waiting for the woodcock and the grouse, and you talk about hunting with your father and his father—you are more at one than any slogan of brotherhood could make you, even though he is the master and you are the man. That is not to mention when rich and poor fall to their knees at Mass.

The people of the Vendée were hard-working peasants whose "backward" ways the Parisians scorned. They loved the Church. Their sons became the broad-backed priests who could walk ten miles through wet country to give the oil of comfort to the dying. So they rose in rebellion against the party that pretended to speak for them. They did not want the Church reduced to a mockery. They did not want their king beheaded. And the republicans in Paris mustered an army to assist those peasants *to their graves*. For a while the brave peasants inflicted embarrassing defeats upon the legions of the new and enlightened future. Then the enlightened struck back with an overwhelming force, including German mercenaries. The massacre of the Vendée began, taking a quarter of a million lives.

Bearing witness to truth

In a world without God, men prey upon one another like monsters of the deep. No restraint, no mercy; blood for drink, or fuel; skulls smashed like eggshells for frying secular omelets. The 20th century stands as evidence. So too the Vendée.

Jacques looked at the shore toward Saint-Nazare. Along its wide bends the Loire had frozen. The town was on fire. How had it come to this? A year ago he had swung on the rope of the church bell to toll the Christmas Mass at midnight. He had heard of the goings-on in Paris, but that was another world. He and his brothers had no thought of bloodshed. Jacques knew how to swing a sickle, not a sword. His hands were thick with calluses round the thumb and under the four fingers. He knew how to trench a field, how to graft slips of sweet apples onto a tougher trunk, and when to stop what he was doing to say the Angelus. There was not one blessed place for political theory in all of his mind and body.

The water was now above their ankles, and the barge spun slowly in the vagaries of the current. When he faced east again, Jacques could see the flare-lit gleam of a rifle. There were soldiers upstream, on the watch, lest someone on the barge should try something.

"My sons," said the priest, "it will be only a little while now. *Confiteor Deo omnipotenti*," he began, and there came the quiet voices of the others in the barge, the bass of old men, the piping tenor of lads who were sprouting the first down of manhood on the chin, praying in the ancient language of the Church. At *mea culpa, mea culpa, mea maxima culpa*, they clenched their fists by force of habit, but did not beat them upon the breast. Their arms were bound. Jacques had lost sensation in his feet. What did that matter? "*De profundis clamavi ad te, Domine*," said the priest, and the men replied as one, "*Domine, exaudi vocem meam*." And so on till the end of the Psalm. Jacques heard a woman crying from the shore, and thought of his mother.

The priest gave them absolution. One of the men suddenly shook violently, causing the barge to rock and take on more water. The westward end tipped and sank. "*In manus tuas commendo spiritum meum*," said the priest, and Jacques repeated it in his mind as the waters closed over them.

Terrible as an army with banners

The Vendée was put down, and the French Revolution triumphed, so it seemed. The history of the world that men write is not the history as is written in the Book of Life. We do not know how many boys from the Vendée are robed in white, whole squadrons of Saints-Jacques and Saints-Étiennes. We do not know how the Lord will call us to testify to the truth, but in the end there is no evasion. You will volunteer for the army of God, or you will be conscripted into the ranks of the enemy.

The people of the Vendée gave their blood for their traditions, their king, and the Church. How will we respond when the call comes? Voltaire, grandfather of the revolution, cried out, "*Ecrasez l'infâme!*"—tear down the unspeakable thing! Nothing has changed. As long as Mass is said in the world, there will be howls against the Church, as if she were the only thing between man and his liberation—liberation, as it will always prove, into slavish vice on earth, and the bondage of the lost below. Innocence itself will be a crime. For it is not hatred that most animates her enemies, but fear.

VIVA CRISTO REY!

❧❧❧❧❧❧

Atheists often say that religion is the source of all the evil in the world, and behave as if they believed it. They never tell us what they think is the source of all the evil *in themselves.*

I'm looking at a photograph taken in Mexico City, November 23, 1926. It's a police compound, outdoors. Snow lies on the rough logs of the wall. To the right stands a man in military uniform, a saber slung at his side. To the left a man is kneeling, his hands pressed together and raised to his lips in prayer. He is handsome and slight of stature, in the prime of manhood. He is dressed in a dark business suit, but if he had had his choice, he would be wearing the outlawed cassock and clerical collar. He is Father Miguel Pro, s.j., and he is about to be executed by firing squad.

Father Pro was accused of taking part in an attempt to assassinate Álvaro Obregón, who with Plutarco Elías Calles formed a tag-team of president-dictators, with Obregón newly elected to the office he had held ten years before. Calles and Obregón hated the Church and persecuted her with a relentless energy that would do credit to an apostle—held in check sometimes by political necessities and not by mercy or second thoughts. Father Pro was innocent, according to the testimony of the would-be assassin himself. He was a man of peace, tending to the needs of the widows and orphans of *los Cristeros*, the soldiers of Christ who were fighting the secular despots. It didn't matter. Let Obregón himself tell us why:

> *We know what to do when an ant bites us: we don't look for the ant…we get a pan of boiling water and throw it on the ant hill. When a scorpion bites us we get a lantern and look for it; and if we find another scorpion, we don't let it live just because it hasn't bitten us; we kill it because it can poison us with its venom, too.*

So Blessed Miguel Pro was led to his death. At the moment of execution, he forgave his enemies and extended his arms in the form of a cross, crying out, *Viva Cristo Rey! Long live Christ the King!* Thirty thousand mourners thronged the streets for his funeral.

Fear and loathing

We crush a scorpion because we fear and loathe it. Reason hardly comes into play. Such is the fear and loathing that Christ's Church arouses. We should never underestimate it.

Catholic priests, said the Mexican consul to the United States, had fought against human

progress and Mexican independence from the beginning. When the Mexican bishops suspended religious services to protest hostile laws that violated
freedom of speech and religion, President Calles
mocked them and said it was so much the better, because the work of eradicating Christianity
would proceed more quickly. Religion is for the
poor and the ignorant, and keeps them so. Such
is the song the illuminati have sung since Voltaire,
hardly caring to hide their contempt for the poor
whom they claim to love.

The anti-Catholic laws were many and insid-
ious, some of them written into the nation's radically secular constitution. Governors could limit
the number of priests allowed to preach in their
states: in Tabasco, one for every thirty thousand
people, and only if those priests *were married and
over forty years old*. Seminaries were shut down.
Spanish-born priests were deported. Religious education for primary school children was prohibit-
ed, even if given outside of school hours. Priests
could not speak on political matters, even as citizens in the public square. The government seized
Catholic orphanages and schools, though most
of the Church's real property had been plundered
long before, when Mexico won her independence
from Spain. In many places it was easier to find
a whore to lie with than a priest to baptize your
child.

Most Americans found the Mexican business baffling, not in keeping with their own progressive view of liberty and their still strong understanding of the central role of religion in the common good. Most, that is, who were not anti-Catholic Klansmen. Prominent Catholics, including William F. Buckley, father of the famous journalist, tried to enlist American support for the rebels, the Cristeros who had finally resorted to armed rebellion. That part of the story is intricate and impossible to reduce to clear saints and villains. The Vatican itself—and that included the never-timid Pius XI—doubted the Cristeros' hope for success, and though it decried the laws as abominable, sought some *modus vivendi* with Calles and Obregón. The Coolidge and Hoover administrations kept a wary distance.

Damned for her virtues

I now hear apologists for Calles crying, "But the Church was worldly and corrupt!" Let's be honest. The Church is never hated for being worldly. Mocked, but not hated. The Church is *hated* not for her vices but for her virtues, which are transcendent, and which put the poor old world to shame. Had Jesus been but a worldly man, his shoulders would never have borne the cross. If the Church would capitulate to the latest demands of the world, then the world would leave it alone—because then the Church, like an inoffensive worm, would not be worth killing.

The Catholic Church in Mexico, long *before* the anti-religious revolution that brought Calles to power, had been a force for liberty and for the welfare of the poor. I'm referring not only to the many works of charity that the Church has always and everywhere performed. Catholics began to take seriously the exhortations of Pope Leo XIII in *Rerum Novarum* (1891), and various Mexican Catholic congresses were pressing for trade unions and guilds, tax-exempt credit cooperatives, free schools, better conditions for sharecroppers and Indians, and even, in exchange for indemnities, the expropriation of large tracts of land held by too few, to be parceled among farmers of the lower classes.

People who have the common good in mind must welcome the vigorous action of the Church. That used to be the attitude of politicians in the United States. This was not the attitude of Calles and Obregón and the "Constitutional" forces they led. I'm looking now at a photograph of Calles. He bears an uncanny resemblance to Stalin, with his mustache, square jaw, heavy brows, and craggy cheeks. The resemblance is more than facial. They were thugs in political garb, mob bosses come to great power; they hated the Faith that had nurtured them; they turned the army against their political enemies; they employed brutal torture and concentration camps; they considered themselves harbingers of a glorious national future, looking on the past with scorn. They were willing to shed the blood of mere farmers, who in Mexico made up the large majority of the Cristeros.

A Church militant

One more photograph. It's a semi-arid middle of nowhere, with tall grass and a few skinny trees. A handsome baldacchino stands in the background, partly hidden by the flag of the Cristeros. A priest in full vestments is giving the Eucharist to a long line of kneeling men. Two soldiers in boots assist him. A second line of men, facing the first line, can be seen in the foreground. The nearest figure is of a powerfully built youth, all in white. These men were willing to fight for the freedom of the Church.

Who were they? All armed struggles attract their share of the violent and ambitious. But the Cristeros had no aims for personal power. Most came from the countryside. They were not rich. Many had grown up in the Catholic Association of Mexican Youth, studying the lives of Catholics like Daniel O'Connell, who fought for Irish independence. They learned, as one of them said, that this life demands a soldier's determination. It demands manhood and self-mastery. We conquer by dying. One of their leaders, Anacleto Flores, an admirer of the works and deeds of Gandhi, preached that all of Mexican life had to be leavened by the teachings of the Church; he rejected secularism out of hand. A few were patriots who simply did not want their nation governed by madmen, and occasionally that patriotism would lead them back into the Church.

No young man says, "I want to grow up to be lukewarm." Who knows what the Church's fortunes will be in the west, so much more hostile to the faith it has lost than it ever was to the faith it had not yet attained. We may be facing a long Lent. But forty days or forty years or four hundred years, we must never give in. We must never say, "We have no president but Caesar!" We must never patronize our Lord, and toss him a scrap of Sundays and pious sentiments. He is our King or he is nothing. *Viva Cristo Rey!*

౧౩ ౧౩ ౧౩

This essay is indebted to David Bailey's fine history of the Cristeros rebellion, *Viva Cristo Rey!*, 1974.

GRAVE, WHERE IS THY STING?

※･❧✦❧･※

With how great a cloud of witnesses are we surrounded! cries the author of the poetic Letter to the Hebrews. What painter ever touched his canvas with so vast an array of human faces, each distinct, himself and no other, and yet in each, old man and youth, maiden and grandmother, king and peasant, the countenance of the Lord Jesus shining forth! Such are the saints of God.

The scene is Seville, 1662. Two men are in conversation. I know only two places where men so opposed in character would be next to one another. One is a graveyard. The other is the Church. The older man is the painter Bartolome Esteban Murillo. Beneath his serious bearing and solid build lies a soft and gentle soul. He came from a large, happy family, he studied art, and after a very little travel he settled down in his beloved home of Seville. For years he has been Spain's greatest painter of religious art. He can do nothing tragic, nothing harsh. Dante's *Inferno* is not in him. His realism is touched with kindness, so that when he paints beggars or street children, they may not be beautiful but they win us with their life and their spirit. No one ever painted the faces of children so well. When he turns to Scripture or the saints, there's a spark of delight in him, a kindness that ensures that whatever he does, it will not quite be like anything we have seen before. Look at his prodigal son. There's the father we expect, his arms flung wide and servants with fine robes for the boy to wear; but our eyes turn to a little white dog in the foreground, leaping for joy. If only we were all as faithful to God as our dogs are to us!

The other man is only thirty-five, but he has been through a hell of his own making. He is Miguel Mañara, known with horror and admiration as the living "Don Juan" of legend. He spent his youth, when not at war, seducing a thousand women and slaying their jealous husbands and angry fathers. Then he met Geronima, the only woman he ever loved, and took her as his wife, returning to Seville, whose people were not glad to have him back. But he had changed. It wasn't only that he settled down. He turned inward: he saw strange warning visions. When his wife died suddenly, he devoted the rest of his life to prayer and strenuous works of piety. He begged to become a member of the Brotherhood of Charity, founded to give a decent burial to executed criminals and the indigent. Only in the Church would we find such a thing; secular man knows nothing of such kindness.

The brotherhood admitted Mañara, and he soon became its *mayor*, its chief. Murillo was one of the brothers. Mañara wanted to expand the brotherhood's work; and Murillo would be a part of it: a killer redeemed, and a man of peace.

The poor deserve our best

"Senor Murillo," I imagine the younger man saying, his face handsome, though creased with dissipation and suffering, "I want us to do more than bury the dead. That's only one of the seven works of mercy. We might do the other six also."

"As private persons, Mayor, many of us do these already."

"Yes, but the *Hermandad* is more. Come and see." And Mañara motions towards a window looking out over the streets of Seville.

For better and for worse, there was no state welfare department. The Church was the mother of the poor, and the hearts of her truest children were their shelter. *The poor you will always have with you*, said Jesus, and Seville proved it. Spain had suffered a bad year of the plague, and in its wake there were even more homeless people than usual, and more orphans on the streets.

Murillo looked down and saw three ragged boys in an alley. Their clothes were filthy. One of the boys was chewing a crust of bread, his shirt torn and falling about his chest. His dog sat beside him, hoping to get some. His companions sat sprawling on the cobblestones. The trousers of one boy were torn up to the knees, and the painter could see the soles of his shoes worn through. A broken jar and a basket of onions lay nearby.

The boys were playing dice.

"What do you have in mind, Mayor?"

"I want to turn the church of the Brotherhood into a hospital. And I want you, the greatest painter in Spain," said Mañara with a touch of his old suavity, "to grace it with six works of mercy. The seventh, you know, we already have." For behind the altar of their Church of the Holy Charity stood a Baroque masterpiece by Pedro Roldán, of the burial of Christ, a polychrome sculpture emerging from a painting of Calvary and framed, as if in a theater, by the gilt pillars and canopy of the architecture roundabout.

Our bodies were fashioned by God as fit tabernacles for his image and likeness, and even in death they are precious and to be treated reverently. *The Son of Man has nowhere to lay his head*, said Jesus, and that was true also on Good Friday, when our Lord had to be buried in a borrowed tomb, hewn out of rock for the rich and pious Joseph of Arimathea. To bury a poor man with honor is to repeat Joseph's loving deed.

"Our hospital," the Mayor continued, "will house the sick and the poor, and give them food and drink and clothing."

"What about the children, Mayor?" The game had broken up and the boys were scuffling, while the dog barked and the onions rolled here and there.

"The children we bring in, we will teach," said the Mayor.

The one thing needful

If you leave a child in a cold white institution to be fed and clothed by functionaries, but not loved, he will not thrive. Modern man is good at building cold white institutions: schools, hospitals, housing complexes, and hospices. We are not cheap with the poor, except in what people need most, which is love. Then we are as tight-fisted as Scrooge. But when the poor were cared for in the Hospital of Charity in Seville, they were granted many a grace, not least of which was the work of Murillo.

He gave the hospital eight paintings, according to Don Miguel's instructions. We are to visit prisoners, as the angel visited Saint Peter and released him from his chains. We are to house the homeless, as Saint John of God did, carrying the poor man on his back; that also applies to travelers, as Abraham welcomed the three young men and showered them with hospitality. We are to give drink to the thirsty, as Moses did when he struck the rock in the desert. We are to clothe the naked, as the loving father did when his scape-grace son returned from the far country. We are to tend to the sick, as Jesus healed the paralytic at the pool, and as Saint Elizabeth of Hungary did during the Black Death, caring for people whom no one else would approach. Murillo could never do anything macabre, so the focus in his painting of Saint Elizabeth is a basin over which the good queen has a small boy leaning, while she cleans his hair of lice; another boy in the background is scratching his head with one hand and his chest with the other. The whole is surmounted by a dome of deep blue, like sapphire.

So are seven of the paintings. Let's dwell a little on the eighth. We are to feed the hungry, as Jesus fed the crowds with the five loaves and two fishes. Murillo's treatment of the miracle is quiet and mysterious. The sky is darkening, and the crowds fade far into the background, hill after distant hill. In the foreground we see Jesus seated and the Apostles around him, a wicker basket at his feet. He is blessing the loaves. To the right of Jesus, almost in the center, stands a boy with two large fish in his arms. He is striding forward and looking up into the face of Saint Peter, to whom he is offering the fish. *Feed them yourselves*, Jesus had said to the Apostles, who did not know how they could do it, but this boy—may he enjoy a special glory in heaven—came forth with his basket of food.

That suggests another sense in which the poor need love. They are not our clients. They are our brothers and sisters, who need also to be able to shower their love upon us. The clasp of a hand goes both ways.

That was what the painter and the penitent gave to the poor of Seville. Four of Murillo's eight paintings still stand there; the others are copies, because modern man buries art in morgues for culture that are called "museums," so that if you are in Ottawa, Washington, Saint Petersburg, or London, you may see at great trouble what people who had not a coin in their pockets once saw to their comfort as they looked up from their prayers.

And when they lay dying, they need not stare at the pocked white tiles of a drop ceiling, and listen to the cold alarm of a machine; they could look upon holiness, and they might hear, from the priest assisting them at their departure, the words of promise which draw the poison from sickness and the sting from death.

☙ ☙ ☙

HILDEBRAND THE GREAT

Somewhere in the marginalia of my facsimile copy of a Calvinist Bible, there's a gloss that gives a name to one of the apocalyptic creatures of prophecy. I'm not sure whether it was Gog or Magog or the beast with the number 666, but the commentator duly notes that the sacred author had foreseen "that devilish Hildebrand," whom Catholics honor as Pope Saint Gregory VII.

Why "that devilish Hildebrand"? Let's turn to one of the most famous moments in medieval history.

The scene is Canossa, a castle on a bare rock perched high in the Apennines of northern Italy. It's held by a woman of immense political accomplishment, the countess Matilda of Tuscany. She herself would merit an epic novel; a founder of churches and the supporter of reforming abbots, bishops, and popes; a learned woman who corresponded with her close friend Saint Anselm; the aunt of Godfrey of Bouillon, who would one day free Jerusalem from the Turks; and the commander of armies holding every mountain pass between Lombardy and Rome. She was not to be taken lightly.

With her is Hildebrand, now Pope Gregory. He is much older than she, but no less determined to assert the independence of the Church and the pope's right to appoint bishops and abbots, so that men of God govern dioceses and abbeys, not men of the world, trading in ecclesiastical offices just as their secular brothers traded in gold and land and armies.

"Why," you might ask, "would a worldly man give up half his manhood to be a bishop, rather than marry and become the progenitor of a powerful family?" Ah, but such men had no intention of forgoing the pleasures of the bedchamber and the prerogatives of fatherhood. "Men must live in the world!" said the German bishops in disbelief, when Gregory commanded them to give up their concubines and to cease celebrating the sacraments if they had obtained their positions by simony—putting the Holy Spirit up for auction. It's the old song.

A king in bare feet

There's one more figure in the scene. It is the Holy Roman Emperor, Henry IV. But he is not inside the castle. He is outside: barefoot, in the snow, in the dead of winter.

An old jest has it that the Holy Roman Empire was neither an empire nor Roman nor holy. There's a lot of truth to that. The emperor was a feudal Germanic lord who held court in Milan or Sicily or the Calabrian town of Cosenza, but hardly ever in Rome. If the Church was fortunate, the emperor might lead a crusade; if not, he'd set himself up as a rival to the pope in everything, with bishops as his chess pieces, and plenty of soldiers for pawns. Against him an aged pope had to rely upon military allies or the often dubious loyalty of his bishops—or, as Gregory did, his spiritual authority and his reputation for sanctity.

When the young Henry first ascended the throne, Gregory urged him not to impede him in his aim to clear out the rat-nests of corruption in a Church that had gotten commandeered by the half-pagans of the north—not to say that France and Italy were much better. As usual in such cases, Gregory had the great support of common people, who do not actually admire prelates with fine horses who go out hunting and whoring. Henry broke his promise. He wanted creatures of his own in charge of the monasteries and dioceses. *He* would "invest" them, giving them their croziers and placing the miters on their heads.

Gregory wrote to him several times, warning him, recalling him to his promise, but to no avail. So he excommunicated the emperor. This meant that Henry's subordinates were released from their vows of obedience, and the common people looked upon it as a curse. So when other German dukes began to move and Henry was at the end of his rope, he went as a pilgrim to Canossa, in the garb of a penitent, to beg absolution from the pope. Gregory was wary of the emperor's motives. I doubt very much that Matilda wanted anything other than to put Henry behind lock and key, and crush his army while she had it at a disadvantage. But Gregory was a man of God. He allowed Henry to humble himself *for three days* in that snow, and then he took him in and lifted the excommunication. After which Henry returned to his old ways, betraying the pope again. Saint Gregory ended up dying in exile from Rome.

Where is your treasure?

"I don't understand," you say. "The emperor wanted as bishops men who were liars and lechers in shepherd's clothing. What did the annotator in your Bible object to?"

Remember what Jesus says about God and mammon. No man can serve two masters. You will love the one and hate the other, or hate the one and love the other. Those words bear upon what we believe to be the relationship between our spiritual and our secular heads on earth. To whom do we owe our ultimate allegiance here? Is it the pope, or is it the king? Is it the Church, or is it the nearest and biggest human creation, the state?

I'm not going to specify just what in our lives belongs more fittingly and immediately to this province or that. I'm not going to engage in theories of governance, which were not on Henry's mind anyway. The question is of order.

A Henry IV comes your way, clapping you on the back, asking your advice on how to settle that uprising in Thuringia, and congratulating you for your shrewdness and courage. After the flattery he comes to the point. "The pope, you know, thinks," or "the Church, as much as we love her, still," and then he asks you to choose the world instead, in just this one little regard. An unborn child here, a boy whose manhood was perverted there, a dash of heresy for intellectual spice; waving the flag for your fatherland, whatever. You will make friends in high places. People will speak well of you.

There it is. Plenty of popes before Gregory had shrugged. Gregory could have done the same, and then died fat and comfortable in Rome. The call to treachery comes in many shapes and all the colors of the rainbow. When it comes to punishing the Church, any stick will do—or any sot of a tyrant, like Henry VIII. Men prefer slavery to the state, if the state permits them some of their favorite vices, to the glorious liberty of the children of God. Do people who choose the state want the Church to be pure? Not at all. They are gladdened by the sight of corruption there. It gives them their excuse. They *want* priests to marry, not because they care about priests, but because celibacy and purity are reproaches to a worldly life. They will say that Gregory insisted that priests be celibate because he wanted Church lands to stay in the control of the Church, rather than being passed along as inheritances. Thus is the Church damned both ways. When churchmen treated the Church as rich men treat their estates, the world scoffs and calls them greedy; and when a Gregory demands that they no longer do so, the world scoffs and says that *the Church* is greedy. Nothing will please the world but the reduction of the Church to irrelevance. We should be accustomed to this by now.

Another burning brand

Hildebrand, that fiery and holy man with the German name, was born in Italy. So was another Hildebrand, whom I'd like to mention here, because where one is praised, so should the other be.

The Hildebrand I am thinking of now, Dietrich von Hildebrand, the son of an aristocratic sculptor, was born in Tuscany, and spoke Italian as his native language. His family was not religious, though his parents instilled in him a love for beauty, both artistic and intellectual. He grew up a lively young man filled with enthusiasm for the truth, and that led him, in his university years, into the Catholic Church.

When Adolf Hitler seized Austria, the man first on his list to kill was Dietrich von Hildebrand, who had inveighed since 1921 against Nazi paganism and their filthy hatred of the Jews. He, too, like his namesake more than eight hundred years before, had to flee from his homeland and all that he held dear. He too, like his namesake, loved the Church. He, too, grew old in a time of troubles. When the Church's enemies had fooled those who should have stood firm for her freedom and her precious treasure of truth—enemies who wanted the Church to become more like the world rather than the world being leavened by the Church—this modern-day Hildebrand said that it was like a Trojan Horse entering the City of God. He has left us countless works of philosophy and theology, most of them yet to be translated from his second language, German.

Two burning brands, afire with holy love. Who will be the third?

ာ ာ ာ

Traveling
to Unknown Shores

⁓⁓⁓⁓

"**B**lack Robe," said a young man, resting his oar on his knees and looking out over a vast stretch of sluggish water, islands, willows, and wild vines studded with grapes not yet bigger than peas, "we must be drawing near to the great river now. The Mother of God has protected us as you said."

For it was not easy for Father Jacques Marquette and Louis Joliet to persuade the five other men to go with them. They were *métis*, sons of French men and Indian women. From the French they had learned the Catholic faith, but from their own people they had heard tales of the wild river we call the Wisconsin, thick with evil spirits, whirlpools, and falls, not to mention bizarre formations of rock carved out by the last "lap" of the retreating glaciers.

If you're a French Canadian, you likely have native blood in you, and that's because the French were never so standoffish or hostile towards the Indians as the English further south were. When Lewis and Clark, nearly a hundred and fifty years later, went on their famous expedition to the northwest and the Pacific Ocean, they availed themselves of the experiences of a Shoshone woman named Sacagawea. That showed what white men and Indians could do when they acted in concert. What's forgotten is that Sacagawea was not their interpreter and guide. That was her husband, a French fur trader named Toussaint Charbonneau. A rover like him would naturally pick up quite a few of the native tongues.

Charbonneau was more of a rascal than a Catholic. He was a distant echo of the French missionaries who traveled through Canada and around the Great Lakes to bring to the savage nations, ever at war with one another, the knowledge of the Prince of Peace. Jacques Marquette was such a man. He could speak six native languages, often making mistakes and causing the women and children who taught him to burst out into happy laughter. The tall young Black Robe was a beloved and respected man. The Indians saw how hard he worked, and how he had given up all that makes life sweet to come live among them and teach them of their Father-God in heaven. He had arrived in New France seven years before, in 1666, and had been sent west to establish outposts of faith in geographically critical places, for instance along the Saint Mary's River, draining Lake Superior into Lake Huron, at which natural trading center they built the mission of Sainte-Marie-du-Sault.

Then Marquette heard from some Illinois Indians of a great river, the "Mesippi," that flowed far south into the sea. Could it be true? If it was, which sea? The Atlantic? The Gulf of Mexico? Might it even be the sea that could take ships to China?

Marquette and Joliet had to find out. If they could claim the river and its lands for France, they could evangelize the Indians in the Catholic faith and block the English from pressing west and encircling them. Both priest and layman cared for the salvation of souls, and both layman and priest were loyal to the crown of France.

The mighty river

Let these men not be mere names in history books. Marquette had left his beloved home expecting never to return. He knew of the brutal deaths of Jean de Brebeuf and his companions, and he hoped in his heart that God would grant him the gift of such a death. At the best, preaching among the Indians was slow and discouraging. Some of the tribes would pride themselves on being the Black Robe's best disciples, but if the priest had to leave them for some time, they would revert to their old ways. So Father Marquette rebuked the Hurons once, on the very day when they were welcoming him back to the mission at La Pointe du Saint-Esprit, telling them that "the intercourse which they have so long had with the infidels had nearly effaced from their minds all vestiges of religion."

The Hurons thought about that and were abashed, and told the Black Robe that they would work harder in the future.

Then there was the poor food, mainly game and corn, and the bitter winters and mosquito-ridden summers; rough housing, always the threat of violence from an enemy tribe like the Iroquois; the boulder-field of language; and physical exertions that only men of great stamina could long endure. And for what cause? To bring the Gospel to our brothers.

See, then, a few birch-bark canoes, seven men living by what they could shoot on the shores or hook from the water, lugging the canoes from the headwaters of the Fox River to the Wisconsin. They were utterly alone and not at all sure of what they were about to do. But Marquette encouraged them: "Let us kneel together in this vast wilderness and commend ourselves to the Mother of God. We will ask her today, and every day, to intercede with her Son to protect us and guide us safely through this perilous journey."

Finally on June 17, 1673, the explorers reached the confluence of the Wisconsin and the Mississippi, with bluffs four hundred feet high on the far side. They entered the mighty river,

Marquette wrote, "with a joy that I cannot express." Marquette kept careful notes, drawing a map for future missionaries, using an astrolabe to record the latitudes, and describing the plants and animals of the countrysides they passed. He was the first European to describe the buffalo.

They continued downriver. They passed the mouth of the Missouri, which when it empties into the Father of Waters has traveled 2,400 miles. They passed the far more dangerous mouth of the Ohio, which at its confluence more than doubles the Mississippi's bulk, and causes it to bend in a great oxbow, turning north and then doubling back upon itself. They reached the mouth of the Arkansas, where they began to see Indians with firearms, who must have encountered the Spanish. Fearing capture—not by Indians, but by their fellow Europeans—and loss of the fruits of their labor, they turned back, paddling upriver all the way to the Illinois, where they took a shortcut toward home by way of Lake Michigan. The entire journey took two years and covered some three thousand miles. Marquette is justly called the Discoverer of the Mississippi.

What it was all about

A reporter was once accompanying Mother Teresa as she cleaned the ulcerous sores of a dying man. The stench was overpowering. "I wouldn't do that for a million dollars," said he.

"Neither would I," said Mother Teresa.

What earthly reward did Father Marquette expect? None, not even the pleasant confidence that he had made many friends who would remember him as their benefactor. Philanthropists do not do what Marquette did. There's no glory in it, nor even much of what the philanthropist would call success. And what is a philanthropist, but a disgruntled man who tries to be a Christian without Christ?

Two days after their arrival at the Mississippi, Marquette and Joliet noticed footprints on the shore. What should they do? What else? Marquette had written of "the blessed necessity of exposing myself for the salvation of all these peoples." So he and Joliet followed a path till they came upon the camp of some Peoria Indians.

Four elders approached the Black Robe in silence. Father Marquette said that they had come in peace. The elders led him to the chief, who broke out in delight, "How beautiful is the sun, O Frenchman, when you have come to visit us! All our village awaits you."

That evening, after they had eaten and had smoked the peace-pipe, Father Marquette spoke.

"I announced to them," he wrote, "that God, who had created them, had pity on them, inasmuch as, after they had been so long ignorant of him, he wished to make himself known to all the peoples." Every true missionary repeats the message of the angels: "I bring you good tidings of great joy."

"Never has the earth been so beautiful," replied the chief, "or the sun so bright as today." The Black Robe, he said, knew "the great spirit who has made us all," and spoke to him, and heard his word. "Beg him to give me life and health, and to come and dwell with us, in order to make us know him."

Father Marquette never would return to the Peorias. The journey broke his health. He died on the return, at one of his old missions on bare Mackinac Island, on May 18, 1675. He was only thirty-seven years old.

"Now he belongs to the ages," they said at the death of Lincoln. It's a fine thing to say of someone who has attained glory in the world. Jacques Marquette does not belong to the ages. He belongs to eternity.

Ȿ Ȿ Ȿ

If you wish to read more about this holy man, I recommend the book that has served me well, *Jacques Marquette*, by Joseph P. Donnelly, s.j.

WHOM YOU MUST RESIST,
FIRM IN THE FAITH

❦

It is July 25, 1934. The scene is the chancellery of Austria. A man whom historians have not done justice lay on the floor, bleeding to death, while his Nazi executioners looked on in cold delight. He asked for a doctor. They refused. He asked for a priest, for the last rites. They refused. Two of the captured guards came to him and tried to stanch his bleeding with a bandage. He thanked them, and said, "I never wanted anything other than peace. We were never the aggressors. We were always forced to defend ourselves. May God forgive them."

The man was the Catholic chancellor of Austria, Engelbert Dollfuss. His words are recorded in the memoirs of the great Dietrich von Hildebrand, a part of which has now been published as *My Battle Against Hitler*.

But Dollfuss is characterized as "controversial" and "authoritarian"—a martyr at the hands of the Nazis!

Who else then fought the Nazis with such determination? As early as 1921, the young von Hildebrand was hated in Germany for saying that the invasion of Belgium had been "a horrible crime," and that the Nazi concept of race was foolish and wicked and utterly incompatible with Catholicism. Did he then win the hearts of Catholics for saying so? No more than Dollfuss has won the hearts of historians. This warrants consideration.

No compromise with falsehood

Some Catholics sought to influence Nazism from within, believing that its nationalism could be respected in part; but von Hildebrand saw through it. Nor had he any patience with puerile contempt for the Chosen People, the Jews. Where were the western statesmen and intellectuals during the twelve years it took for Hitler to come to power? Maybe busy dallying with eugenics of their own, or unwilling to condemn what claimed to be the wave of a collective future. Maybe they were not keen to perceive Hitler's threat to the Faith that is the life of European culture, because they had given up that faith, or had allowed it to become a conditional faith: not in what Jesus did or said, but in what they made believe he *would have done and would have said*, had he been a good socialist among them.

Engelbert Dollfuss was not an ambitious man. He jested that his growing deafness was a gift of God, because then he could retire sooner. He was a devout Catholic who wanted to see

Catholic Austria standing free, independent, the voice of old Europe against the madness of Nazism and the inhumanity of collectivism. When he became chancellor in 1932, Austria bristled with socialist and nationalist parties, armed with militias and eager for violent revolution to get their way. Dollfuss saw that the ordinary machinery of democracy would prove worse than useless: the Nazis wanted disarray in Austria. So in 1933 he dissolved parliament and established the Patriotic Front, to unite all who sought first the independence of their nation and resistance against the Nazis.

He and Austria would be almost alone: the League of Nations tried to mollify the Nazis, and radicals of all stripes cried out against his policies. Dollfuss knew that Mussolini in Italy favored an independent Austria, and (at that time) considered Hitler a disgrace. Dollfuss enlisted *il Duce*'s support, though he knew that fascism was another form of the evil of the collective. Historians will not forgive him for that, either.

Yet von Hildebrand says that Dollfuss stood like David against Goliath. The comparison is apt. Dollfuss was called the "Milli metternich," standing barely five feet tall. He didn't take himself seriously; he did take truth seriously. He saw that politics had to address fundamental questions about the human person, his orientation towards community, and his destiny before God. Franklin Roosevelt, President of the United States when Dollfuss was murdered, could hardly have conducted a sensible conversation with the chancellor about such things. "Hitler," said Dollfuss, "wants to draw on ancient German paganism, but I want to draw on the Christian Middle Ages." I'm trying to imagine how Western darlings like the atheist educator John Dewey, the self-styled prophet H. G. Wells, and the modernist George Bernard Shaw would have scoffed at that. But they were wrong, and Dollfuss was right.

The journal appears

To support Dollfuss and to refute the errors of Nazism and Bolshevism and other plagues, von Hildebrand published a new journal in Vienna, *The Christian Corporative State*. Dollfuss provided the title. He said he wanted to set Austria upon the firm foundation of Pius XI's social encyclical *Quadragesimo anno*. Dollfuss rejected both liberal individualism and the absorption of the individual into the state. The Catholic vision he promoted is no queasy compromise between those two, but something quite different; a way of life based upon the dignity of the human person as made in the image of God *and* oriented towards a life of love among others. He saw the ideal social life in terms of "corporations"—we may think of the

Medieval university, bringing together masters and students. Dollfuss believed that owners and workers had shared interests, and could unite in a corporation to pursue them with justice and charity.

WAS WIR WOLLEN—WHAT WE WANT; that's the bold headline above the mission statement in the journal's first issue. The words are no less meaningful for us now than they were then: "The great teachings of classical Western thought have to be opposed to various false and confused conceptions, to economic materialism and to racial materialism, to liberal individualism and to pagan conceptions of unlimited state sovereignty."

The journal wielded great influence. Franz von Papen, a Catholic Nazi and ambassador to Austria, said that von Hildebrand was a dangerous man: "No one does more harm to us than he." Later he would plot to have the philosopher assassinated. No doubt he was apprised of the murder of Dollfuss. Who knows how many people von Hildebrand saved by his intellectual clarity and courage? Or how many millions might not have met their deaths at places like Dachau, had more Catholics been like Dollfuss and von Hildebrand? Once, when von Hildebrand was visiting his old friend Eugenio Pacelli, the future Pope Pius XII, he asked why Catholic prelates in Germany did not all stand up bravely against the stupidities of

Nazism. Pacelli shook his head sadly. Martyrdom could not be commanded from Rome, he said. Martyrdom had to come from within.

Two witnesses for mankind and the faith

Dietrich von Hildebrand, who had fled his ancestral home and his university in Munich, would soon have to flee Austria also. His father was an aristocrat and a renowned sculptor; the family was related to German composers and conductors; von Hildebrand had studied under the great German phenomenologist Edmund Husserl. He and his wife would leave all that culture behind, with no money in their pockets and no sure prospects for employment, with close calls on trains and at borders, to come to the United States, where he taught at Fordham University—a relentless searcher into the truth, and a humble and loyal son of the Church. Therefore he was ignored by secular academics, and when, in his old age, he warned against intellectual and moral errors entering the Church as if by a new Trojan Horse, he was ignored by many of his fellow Catholics too. But God does not ignore such faith and self-denying courage.

As for Chancellor Dollfuss, von Hildebrand could not understand how one could hate him "who was so noble, so kind, so well-wishing toward everyone, who fought against the Antichrist of National Socialism." The answer is not far to seek. He was hated because he was noble and kind. He was not hated because in 1933 he was compelled to put down a conflict that threatened to erupt into all-out civil war. He was hated because he sought to forgive his enemies, pleading with all men of good will to join him for their country's sake. His life of prayer and submission to the Church earned him no favor with such, just as a similar life now earns you little more than loathing from secular reporters, politicians, and educators—and many of those now, as their counterparts then, will have subordinated their Catholic faith to the spirit of the age.

Let it not be so among us! Truth is truth to the end of time. Be not deceived. No falsehood under the sun is ever really new. What would we have done in the days of Hitler? Ask instead what we are doing now against the massive wrongs and follies and betrayals of this time. Let the diminutive statesman and that philosopher with the heart of a lion instruct us in the way of martyrdom.

ℰ℧ ℰ℧ ℰ℧

Measure, Weight, and Number

⚬☙❦☙⚬

When I tell people that my first love was not poetry but mathematics, they usually knit their brows and wonder what brought about that leap across a chasm. It was no leap. Poetry is a world of meaning rendered in musical order, and mathematics is a world of number and shape, of momentum and direction, of unity and difference and relationship; it too has its streams and trees and branches and leaves, its planets gliding along realms of space curved like a water slide, its singularities at the heart of a bottomless funnel, its surprises, its vistas without end. So God is often portrayed as a geometer, measuring out the world with a compass and saying to the waters, "Thus far shall thy proud waves be stayed."

Plato, that philosopher with the soul of a mystic, had an inscription carved over the archway of his Academy: "Let no one ignorant of geometry enter here." His sense was that meditation upon mathematical objects was a step along the way to the contemplation of the Good. That is because mathematical objects do not change or decay; and what we know about them, we know with certainty. The real existence of a single mathematical object—a number, a curve, an infinite series—is a knife in the heart of materialism. Real knowledge of such is a knife in the heart of sophism and skepticism.

So we shouldn't be surprised to find so many deeply devout men among the greatest of mathematicians. Blaise Pascal, inventor of probability theory, is one of the most penetrating theologians who ever lived. Leonhard Euler was the Johann Sebastian Bach of German mathematics in the 18th century: a devout Lutheran, happily married, with a big brood of children, and possessed of immense creativity and intuition. Bernhard Riemann originally went to the university to become a pastor; his tombstone cites Saint Paul: *All things work together for those who love God*. Georg Cantor, the titan of set theory and discoverer of trans-finite numbers, believed that his work on the nature of infinity demonstrated the necessary existence of God. Kurt Gödel, inspired by Cantor's work, turned his own world-shaking Incompleteness Theorem to account, developing from it a revision of Saint Anselm's proof. Albert Einstein was once asked why he wanted to work at Princeton. "So that I can have lunch with Kurt Gödel," he said.

And there is one more man who ranks with the three or four greatest ever, whose fingerprints are to be found in every branch of mathematics: the devout Catholic Augustin-Louis Cauchy (1789–1857).

Boy genius

Augustin-Louis had advantages that are lacking to young men today. He was never subject to institutional chloroform: he did not go to school during his early years, but was educated by his father, himself a man of impressive learning. Then, at the urging of the elder mathematician and astronomer Joseph-Louis Lagrange (1736–1813), he went to the École Centrale du Panthéon, to study—not math, but classical languages. At age sixteen he began his mathematical studies in earnest, at the École Polytechnique; ability and not age was his passport. His work was so brilliant that Napoleon, who by then had taken over the revolutionary regime—much to the benefit of the conservative Cauchy family—tabbed the young man to be one of his chief engineers at Cherbourg. Napoleon wanted to realize a long-held aim of the French, which was to dredge and enclose the harbor at Cherbourg, building "moles" and jetties and fortified hills to render Cherbourg more useful as a port and impregnable as a military redoubt. The project took many stages, but until recently Cherbourg boasted the largest artificial harbor in the world. Cauchy was nineteen when he began. What are our brightest sons doing at that age now—if their brains have not been soaked in drugs, and their souls in vice?

In his spare time Cauchy was writing papers filled with original work on solid geometry, calculus, and sound waves; I should note that a "paper" proving a subtle and far-reaching conjecture of Fermat would be the equivalent, not in pages but in sheer labor and genius, of writing a fair-sized book in the humanities. But Cauchy was a tireless man, with more than 700 such papers to his name when he died. In any case, the strain and the bad air at Cherbourg wore on his health, so he left the engineering works to become a professor at the École Polytechnique, at age twenty-two.

Politically incorrect

Throughout his professorial career, Augustin-Louis Cauchy was willing to pay for his convictions. His unabashed Catholicism grated on the nerves of his secular colleagues. When the Bourbon dynasty fell in the revolution of 1830, Cauchy did not wait for his colleagues to act, but went into exile along with the king. The next ten years or so found him in Turin, in Prague, then back in Paris. The Italians created a chair in mathematical physics just for him; the French liberals would not be so generous. When Cauchy applied for a position at the Bureau of Longitudes, he was voted down because he would not renounce the legitimacy of the Bourbon kings. For one of his applications to an ordinary post he was rejected by the academicians, forty-two to three. Imagine Einstein applying for a job as an assistant professor at Princeton—or Rutgers—and gaining only three out of forty-five votes. For several years, Cauchy was not even earning any money, and by then he was a married man with a wife and two daughters to support.

When the revolution of 1848 brought Napoleon III to the throne, the new king exempted Cauchy from taking the loyalty oath, and so the great mathematician could live out the rest of his days in France. But that didn't mean that he kept silent about important matters. The French secularists wanted to banish the Church from public life, consigning it to the walls of your home or your parish church. Call it "freedom of worship," 19th-century version, with rigorous restraints upon the free exercise of faith. Cauchy would have none of it. He stood up for the Jesuits when they were attacked. He stood up for the independence of their schools. He stood up for the preservation of the Lord's Day as a day free of labor. He wrote to the pope on behalf of the Irish during the potato famine. He was personally active in works of charity as a member of the Society of Saint Vincent de Paul.

Cauchy was also a close friend of the most potent Jesuit preacher in France, Gustave Xavier de Ravignan. One longs to have been a witness to their conversations: the mathematician and the Jesuit priest, known for his ascetic life, his zeal for souls, and his precise logic in defense of the faith. Of Père de Ravignan they say that his writings are wanting in flights of imagination, but he was a powerful and magnetic presence. Thousands of men flocked to his retreats. I think there is a certain kind of man, pure, exact, relentlessly logical, who is moved less by emotional outbursts than by the brilliant light of reasoning from premises to conclusions. Cauchy was one such, and evidently there were many others.

How firm a foundation

Augustin-Louis Cauchy, France's finest mathematician, was an ardent Catholic. What influence did his faith have on his mathematical work? I'll end this essay with something that mathematicians might appreciate: a conjecture.

Cauchy wrote in the introduction to his most important work, the *Cours d'analyse de l'École royale polytechnique* (1821), that mathematicians before him had committed "sins," and that he was going to correct them. One writer suggests that this language of sin and confession comes out of the Council of Trent. But we do not need to invoke Trent; and there's a better way to understand what Cauchy wanted.

Cauchy had in mind two tendencies among his predecessors. One was to rely on demonstrations that fell short of airtight proof. The other was to consider algebra as a system of abstractions dealing with other abstractions, a self-enclosed language that referred ultimately only to itself. The first "sin" was like a flawed attempt to prove the existence of God; a mind like that of Thomas Aquinas—or Cauchy—would not be satisfied until the proof was rectified.

The second "sin" has implications that are profounder still. Cauchy always insisted that mathematics does in fact refer to really existing things, even if the things are but geometrical figures, like a triangle or a polyhedron. He wanted to give a firm basis to the discoveries made by his predecessors, both by cleaning up their proofs *and* by referring them back, again and again, to realities—though perhaps realities that can be perceived only by the mind.

For God has created *the world*—not an abstract game, but the world—in measure, weight, and number. Augustin-Louis Cauchy saw it, and believed.

ℰℬ ℰℬ ℰℬ

SLAVE OF THE ETHIOPIAN SLAVES

«๛๏๛๖๏๛»

"This book was owned by the happiest man in the world."

Before I tell who wrote that, we might wonder what would justify such a claim. Was the man rich, admired, the father of many children? Did he enjoy the pleasures of the world in moderation, living to a good old age and dying peacefully, as a ripe apple drops softly from the tree?

Saint Peter Claver was none of those things. He could have lived the comfortable life of a wise and kindly teacher at Montesión, the Jesuit college in Palma, on Majorca in the Mediterranean. Think of that for a moment. Fresh salt breezes, palm trees, no snow, no swelter; and Spain, your homeland, a short voyage away.

You could achieve holiness in Palma, too.

The elderly doorkeeper at Montesión did. We honor him as Saint Alonso Rodriguez. Alonso was a widower who gave up his life in the world to join the Jesuits. For twenty years he kept the door; he was the first and immediate servant of all who came to visit Montesión. The world would not now appreciate a man like Alonso, with his childlike humility and docility. But Peter Claver understood him. They became fast friends. It was Alonso who told Claver that the harvest was plentiful in the New World, especially among the poor Africans transported there by the slave ships, and that he should appeal to his superiors to send him. Father Claver, in *his* humility and docility, had balked at urging it too boldly.

They were alike, these two. Alonso's job was utterly mundane, nothing spectacular about being a doorkeeper. But his childlike sweetness and his unceasing life of prayer won the hearts of all who met him. Meanwhile it was said of Peter Claver that he was a novice from first to last. He never questioned a command, so his superiors needed never to worry about who would clean the latrine or the stables. They had only to ask Father Claver.

So he did as Alonso recommended, and two years later he found himself in Cartagena, the swarming slave port on the Caribbean.

Light in darkness

"Hurry, son," says Father Claver, his shoulders bearing one end of a pole upon which are slung big baskets of fresh vegetables, lemons, bread, flasks of wine, bandages, and other necessaries. "They've already arrived! Let's not be late!" His eyes are wide with good cheer, as if he were a boy running to the carnival.

"Yes, Father," says the young Jesuit at the other end of the pole, his knees buckling and his shoulder chafing against the wood. He can hardly keep up.

That was Peter Claver's routine for thirty-five years. Nobody knew how he managed it, since he slept very little and ate only one or two pieces of bread and some fried potatoes each day. Love and holiness were like fire in his veins, giving him a stamina that was supernatural. He did not waste away, or succumb to scurvy from his bad diet, or contract the diseases that riddled the wretches he served.

"Here they are!" he cries, as more than a hundred miserable human beings are led staggering from a ship by their guards.

Imagine the horror. The Africans are naked—men, women, and children. The men are in chains. A third of them died at sea. They were cramped below deck to eat and drink and relieve themselves, stewing in their filth, puking from the stench and the rolling sea, ravaged with dysentery, the men's legs ulcerous from the shackles; blood and mucus soaking the floors; fed nauseating stuff and flogged if they refused to eat it; knowing nothing of what was happening to them or why.

It is the hell on earth that men make for one another.

Then they meet Father Claver.

The slave traders were horrible Catholics, but they let Claver do his work.

He smiled upon the Africans, speaking to them in Angolan Portuguese, using African interpreters for a few other languages, but mainly communicating in the universal human language of gentle touches, to comfort them, soothe them, give them heart.

He fed them the first good food they had had since they were captured. He washed their wounds with wine. He cleaned the filth from their bodies. He bound up their sores. He clothed their nakedness. The stench was so choking that no one but Claver could endure it for more than a few minutes. He didn't notice it, or if he did, he took it as a gift from God.

He kissed them. He sucked the poison from their sores, the way you'd suck the venom from a snakebite—but this poison was from disease and putrefying flesh.

If they could not walk, he carried them. He made carts for the sick so they would not have to hobble along under the lash. To those who were dying he ministered first of all, ready with the water and oil of baptism, if they could be made to understand the merest notion of their sin and of Christ's salvation.

In the days when they were herded into barracks before being sold, Claver would preach the

Gospel, using for illustration a medal of Jesus and Mary that his friend Alonso had given him.

"If the Spanish are in heaven," a native once said, "let me go to hell, so I will not have to see them anymore." He could not have been referring to Peter Claver. The blacks never said, "He is one of our tormentors." They listened to him. Africa had its own horrors, and Africans were sinners too.

Only a love beyond human reckoning could have won their hearts. It is a love that the world does not know how to give, a love the world had never heard of before Christ.

Among the lepers

Peter Claver was not a mere humanitarian. He had no agenda for the social improvement of man. He was consumed with love for the individual, and the more miserable and needy, the more ardent was his love.

The humanitarian does not sit at the bed of a dying man; he gives him morphine to be rid of him most efficiently. But human beings are not objects of efficiency. Jesus would have borne the cross *for one sinner alone*. Was that efficient? He suffered and died for Alonso and Peter and you and me, individually. All of *that*, because he wanted our friendship.

Lepers will flush out the humanitarian from his covert every time. See the grotesque disfigurement;

fingers, noses, ears missing; the glorious human body reduced to clots, cleft and pocked and burst open like rotten fruit. Only a saint would go among lepers. Many of the slaves had contracted leprosy, and were sent to live out their last days in a colony. Claver went among them.

Of course in those days there were no latex gloves, goggles, and antiseptics. We can imagine a very good person in our days on a temporary mission, bolstered with the protections of modern industry, going among lepers, and being satisfied with himself for years after. But Peter Claver did more than to go among them, to perform the necessary medical tasks, and then to leave in a cold sweat of relief. He was eager to go among them. To prove it, he did for them what no humanitarian would ever do. He touched them. He kissed them. He gave them back their dignity as human beings. His actions said, "You do not disgust me. You delight me, you are valuable to me, you need not be embarrassed in front of me. You are my brothers."

He did not run away from the plague. We run away from suffering *as if it were the plague*.

The pursuit of happiness

Father Claver made himself a slave in more ways than one. He placed an African in authority over him, and obeyed his decisions. He would awake in the middle of the night to hear confessions for eight hours, saying Mass in the morning and then Mass again at noon, before taking a drink of water. If one of the Africans was so ill he made the others nauseous, Father Claver lodged him in his own room, giving him his bed while he slept on the floor. People say of a generous man that he would give you the shirt off his back. But Claver would use his own robe to veil the sickest from the sight and smell of others; or let them use it as a pillow, or a cushion to sit on.

Sinners too are lepers. They too need the touch of love.

So I will end this essay with a story. There was a Spaniard who was sentenced to a horrible death for counterfeiting. Father Claver ministered to him in his cell. On the day of the hanging the rope broke, twice, and each time Claver was there to hold the man in his arms. The second time it broke, it must have done its job first, because the man gasped out his last breath while the priest was holding him.

It was that man, not Father Claver, who had written in his prayer book the night before, "This book was owned by the happiest man in the world."

ভ৩ ভ৩ ভ৩

Speaking
the Painful Truth

The two women were finally alone. The room was spartan, with a single wooden bed, a desk, some schoolbooks, fishing tackle kept in a corner, and a couple of skiing poles. A photograph was mounted on the wall, of two tanned young men in a skiff, with the spires of Stockholm in the background. It was a boy's room, but the boy had left home to join the Swedish army. It was May, 1940.

"Sigrid," said her friend Alice, "I have bad news for you." She had given Sigrid a day to rest from her journey across the mountains from Norway, in a truck packed so tight with soldiers and refugees. Sigrid—a middle-aged woman with some heft to her, and a countenance that looked as if she would brook no foolishness—had to sit on the lap of one of the men. The atmosphere in the truck had been tense, with Swedish boys expressing their eagerness to fight alongside the Norwegians against the Nazi invaders, and elder men telling them to shut up. News from the war front was also unrelievedly bad. Hitler had overrun Belgium and the Netherlands, and the

German armies were pushing on toward Paris, the jeweled queen of European civilization.

"Please, tell me quickly," said Sigrid. She had had three children. One, a daughter, had died as a very young woman. Her sons Anders and Hans were still in Norway. The elder, Anders, had a commission as captain in the Norwegian army.

"Your son Anders fell in the fighting at Segelstad bridge. He was brave, Sigrid, so brave," said Alice, trembling. Sigrid, however, set her face like flint. Of Hans, they still knew nothing. A few days later they received a visit from a soldier who had been under Anders' command. The Norwegians had tried to make the Nazi advance northward as costly as possible, taking positions near bridges and mountain passes, and holding off hundreds of Germans with handfuls of men and a few machine guns here and there. Had Norway been made ready for the assault—had there not been Nazi toadies like Quisling in the highest positions in government—Hitler would have regretted sending Germans into that nation of strong, self-reliant, upright, and brave men and women.

"And Anders, you know," said the soldier, "was so incomparably kind." The word he used was *snill*. Sigrid Undset said that the word was untranslatable. It named a virtue—kindness—but with a quiet manner, undemonstrative, reserved; not burdening your victim with your goodness.

Hans arrived shortly after, and he and his mother continued on their flight to freedom, from Sweden to Moscow, from Moscow by a nine-day train ride to Vladivostok, from there to Korea and imperial Japan, from Japan via the *Grover S. Cleveland* to San Francisco.

Who she was

Sigrid Undset, for my money, is the greatest woman novelist who ever lived. Unlike George Eliot, one of her two chief competitors for that distinction, she does not rely upon the structure of Christian morality without the Christian Faith. In her stories set in modern times, Undset shows how frail that morality must be, unless we recognize our personal frailty and our desperate need for the grace of Christ. Eliot (Mary Ann Evans) had lost the Methodist faith she was brought up in; Undset had gained the Catholic Faith she was *not* brought up in. Unlike Jane Austen, her other competitor, she was not the comfortably stationed daughter of an Anglican clergyman, who could therefore take faith for granted and write about Christian morals and manners in the England of her time. Undset, when she entered the Catholic Church, knew she was entering into two thousand years of history, and so her greatest works, the trilogy *Kristin Lavransdatter* and the tetralogy *The Master of Hestviken*, are set in medieval

Norway—Catholic but still with remnants of the old pagan ways. They are national in the best sense: they celebrate the difficult virtues of her people and the beauty of a forbidding land, with its summer so wondrous yet so heartbreakingly short, its wildflowers, its mountains and fjords and ravines, its lonely lichen-topped outcrops of rock, its sudden green valleys, and its brave men wresting the means of life from the rich and cold and dangerous seas.

The contrast between Sigrid Undset's love of country and the pranked-up nationalism of Hitler and his blustering warmongers could not be greater. She despised the Nazis. Other people—not nearly enough—saw their evil; Undset saw also their stupidity and their cowardly ingratitude. For among the invading German soldiers, the Norwegians recognized quite a few whom they had taken into their homes as little boys, back in the famine years after the First World War. She was outspoken about it, and so she, like Dietrich von Hildebrand in Austria, was on the first page of the Nazi list of people to be murdered.

Wherever she went, Sigrid Undset tried to find what virtues she could in the peoples she encountered. Germans, alas, were the exception. She had to fight her hardest to treat that people with forbearance. For her, the essence of the German spirit was expressed in the terrifying fable of *The*

How the Church Has Changed the World

Pied Piper of Hamelin. The "hero" took his vengeance against the ungrateful people of Hamelin by turning their children essentially into *rats*, marching off to their death. I forgive the mother of a fallen son her anger.

Undset held out hope for the great successor of European civilization, the United States. Even if Europe should fall (she was writing in 1941) the United States would carry the torch of that civilization's commitment to brotherhood, equality, and democracy, understood as the natural flowering of the Christian Faith.

Return to the future

That's the name of the book that describes her trek from Norway to the United States. It also describes her hope for the world. The future must be a *return*: a recovery of the Christian Faith in nations that had lost it, and a flourishing of the human good that man experiences as one of the blessings of that faith.

Should Germany be defeated, the victors must resist with all their might the temptations of hatred and vengeance. How hard that would be, Undset shows us in her own person. But, she says, "hatred and thirst for revenge *are* sterile passions." They engender nothing. They only destroy. "The most miserable poverty, the most unthinkable filth and squalor, the indescribable

166

stench of refuse and decomposition which I saw and smelled everywhere in Soviet Russia are surely the fruit of the acceptance by Russia's revolutionary heroes of a hate-consumed old German Jewish writer named Karl Marx and their identification of their future goals with his dreams of revenge against everything that happened to awaken his enmity."

Undset was no sentimentalist. It is true, she was a woman with a woman's eye for the delicate and the beautiful; she is fond of describing flowers, handsome dress, lovely hair; the fine straw-roofed houses of even the poor in Japan; the tasteful Japanese temples; the reverent ceremonies of prayer she witnessed from the worshipers of Shinto. She has a woman's scorn for the garish, grubby, slipshod, and gross: nine days on a Russian train with no running water and no flush toilets; Soviet stores with nothing to sell; water that had to be boiled before you could drink it; Soviet officials content to bury themselves and their petitioners under a mountain of paper. Totalitarian systems fail on their own miserable terms: they deliver poverty instead of wealth, confusion instead of order, misery instead of happiness, family dissolution rather than strength, dependence rather than self-reliance, cowardice rather than courage.

So much the more should the west *return to its roots in the Christian Faith*. That Faith is not an ideology, but the antidote to ideology. It tells the truth about God and man.

Nowadays we construct social policies as if God were irrelevant, and as if everything that the wisest pagans had to say about man, and likewise the Christian Gospels that soar beyond the pagans, could be dispensed with. Yet we pretend that, if we were alive in Germany during the time of Hitler, we would not have gone along with the popular wave of the future, as the Nazis styled themselves. No, we'd have seen through it. Quisling did not. Knut Hamsen, like Undset a Nobel laureate, did not. Undset did. The Faith—uncompromised, uncontaminated with the current prevailing ideologies—gave Sigrid Undset eyes, and heart, and a pen to write words as if etched in stone by fire.

ɷ ɷ ɷ

A GIANT AMONG MEN

※◦◦◎∕◯∖◎◦◦※

One of the benefits of a cold day was that it almost smothered the stench of destruction: parched and sodden beams torn out of homes, barns, mills, churches; human and animal waste in the alleys; death in the fields. The day was very cold. The cardinal stooped to hear the voice of a woman wrapped in black and wearing on her feet only the wooden *sabots* of the poor. It was not only age and his voluntary privations that bowed his back. He had to bow: he was six feet ten inches tall.

"Your Eminence," said the woman, "my son Marcel, my only son, has fallen in the trenches along the Yser."

"My dear daughter, I shall pray for him at Mass."

"Thank you," she said, and hesitated, crumpling a rosary between her hands.

"I'm in no hurry," he said. "God meant for me to be here speaking with you. Do you need food or shelter? What can I do for you?"

"No, no, Eminence," she said, though she had not tasted meat in months. "Marcel was sometimes not the best Catholic. Oh, he went to

Mass, but he was fond of drink, and you know what soldiers are, and—I am afraid."

The cardinal had heard it many times before. "Daughter," he said, "I *do* know what soldiers are. Our soldiers are our saviors. Our Lord never had a hard word for the soldier, and remember what he said, that greater love hath no man than this, than to lay down his life for his friends. Marcel has laid down his life for our poor beloved country, our brave and noble Belgium. He has suffered unto blood. Can we who honor his heroism doubt that God welcomes him with love?"

Kindness did what sorrow could not. The woman wept.

"Pray for his soul, but be confident, hope in God. How powerful is a single perfect act of charity! In all my life I have never done anything more Christlike than what Marcel has done. What are sins against that purifying fire?"

Statesman and patriot

The cardinal sat at his desk. His shelves were stacked with books on chemistry, biology, and physics; volumes from the Fathers and the schoolmen; works of philosophy ancient and modern, in the original languages. A gilt crucifix hung on the wall. When the cardinal felt weary or prone to question the providence of God, he regained his soul's peace by meditating upon the wounds of Jesus.

"Your Excellency," he wrote, "I thank you for attending to my letter, though I am disappointed in your reply. You say you want to bind up the wounds of Belgium. I beg you then to recall the assurances your predecessors gave me in person and in writing, that no Belgian citizen would be conscripted to assist the German army or set to forced labor. Yet your soldiers have in one night, without considering the needs of the families, rounded up two thousand Belgian men and boys and transported them to Germany to work in your factories. If the tears of mothers and children cannot move you, consider the honor of a man's word, and remember that God watches, and he is just.

"You say England has thrust this conscription upon you by her blockade, and you suggest that we blame our ally for our misery. Surely, your Excellency must see that were it not for the German invasion and occupation of Belgium, we would not now be suffering the "unemployment" you use to justify your actions. Who but Germany has destroyed our mills, and who but Germany has deprived us of the raw materials our factories need? Moreover, these "unemployed" men have, by direction of our exiled king and our bishops and priests, obeyed all laws pertaining to public order. They are not at your charge. With the help of men from neutral countries, we have kept them and their families from famine.

"Nor is work merely work, as you know. Every Belgian man in a German factory frees one German man to fight in the army that has ravaged his land and slain his sons and brothers. War, not the alleviation of hardship in Belgium, is the true reason behind the conscription."

The cardinal laid down his pen and buried his face in his hands. "I must not hate," he said. "The baron too is precious in the sight of God. I must not cringe and beg, but I must not hate. Nor may I yield. Right is peace, and right is founded upon order, on justice."

Then he took up the pen once more.

Like a shepherd

A portly man in his forties stood before the cardinal with bills of lading. Food shipments had newly arrived at Ostend. He was a mining engineer and a man of industry. He got things done.

"We meet in the flesh at last," said the cardinal, rising and taking the younger man by the hand. "Words cannot express the debt that all of Belgium, Catholic and Protestant, owes to you—hundreds of thousands of human souls, saved from starvation and exposure."

The man flushed. For his age he had had plenty of adventures, even in wartime—for he was the one man determined to keep his team of Americans and Englishmen and the citizens of Tientsin at the defense of the city during the Boxer Rebellion. They prevailed. Yet he was a man of peace, brought up as a Quaker: *he* did not fire one shot.

"Your Eminence," said this chief of operations for the relief of Belgium, "we all do what is only our duty. God will reward us, we know. But the duty remains, it is pressing, and we must respond." The chief had creases around his eyes; he'd often go several days with only a few hours of sleep.

"They trust you," said the cardinal. Only someone committed absolutely to neutrality could acquire leave to travel behind the German lines. God might well employ a Quaker to save Catholics.

"I want you to know where my heart lies," said the man.

"No need," said the cardinal. "But here," he said, turning toward his desk. "I have reports from priests in Liège, Charleroi, Leuven, and Tournai. You'll see that in the country our most pressing need is for grain, and in the cities it is greens and milk."

"I'll arrange the deliveries accordingly. This last shipment is only three tons, very small, but I have assurances from the United States and from Brazil that much more will soon be on the way."

"Be assured of the eternal gratitude of our people, Mr. Hoover," said the cardinal, "and of my prayers." Then the cardinal and the industrialist shook hands, and each turned again to his wartime tasks.

The mind's journey to God

The cardinal stood among the ruined schools of the Louvain, where he had taught Thomistic philosophy for so long. He was the most eminent Catholic philosopher of his generation, wielding the sword of his mind against philosophical errors in the ascendant—the positivism of Auguste Comte, the materialism of Herbert Spencer, the idealism of Immanuel Kant and his followers. He wrote learnedly on the constitution of the cell, on the nervous system and the organization of the brain, on vegetative and animal life; on the difference between saying that all human knowledge originates in the senses and saying that man knows nothing whatever of what cannot be sensed. His intellect was taller than his frame.

The young men waited for him to speak. These were devout Catholics who knew that the war their brothers were fighting was not the only war; or they were two theaters of the same war—one fought with ideas on behalf of the truth of God and man, and the other with bayonets, grenades, guns, spades, barbed wire, muscle and bone and blood, for the honor and freedom of their Catholic homeland.

"My sons," began Désiré Mercier, Cardinal Archbishop of Malines, "the Lion of Mechlin" in the American press, a man who in insight and charity towered over the cold puritan Wilson, the brutal Bolsheviks, the vindictive Georges Clemenceau, the opportunist Lloyd George— "my sons," he cried, "now above all we need a philosophy that does justice to the intuition that this life is not all there is! The restless spirits of our youth cry for a wisdom that appeals to all that the mind can know. The eternal philosophy is the door to that wisdom. The works of Thomas Aquinas, which I have been blessed to teach for thirty years, are the key to that door.

"The forces of modern inhumanity have battered the walls of our university. They cannot touch the truth, which remains inviolate and pure, as hard and as brilliant as diamond. This truth is human too: for we profess Jesus Christ, the way, the truth, and the life.

"These walls we will rebuild—no doubt of that. It is for you to go forth armed with truth into a world that is confused and dispirited, for without truth there is no charity. My sons," he said, faltering, for the terrible years had taken their toll, "be of good cheer. Quit yourselves like men, be steadfast, never yield to what is easy and worldly and false. Then shall Belgium shine in true glory, and our efforts for her will not have been in vain."

ℰℬ ℰℬ ℰℬ

He Has Lifted up the Lowly

The boys in the loft raised their pure and unearthly voices to the arches above, resounding throughout the vast cathedral: *Semen ejus in aeterno manebit: et sedes ejus sicut sol in conspectu meo, et sicut luna perfecta in aeternum: et testis in caelo fidelis.* It was a simple and solemn melody, at most only four or five notes on a syllable, and the boys had sung it on many another saint's day. The choirmaster had told them what it meant, though a few of the older boys had learned enough Latin to know it by themselves. The evening was cold and their breath rose visibly in the air. But for all that they were cheerful, and could hardly keep from whispering mischievously one to another before Mass was ended.

It was Saint Nicholas' Day, in Salisbury, England—or it could have been Bruges, in Belgium, or Burgos, in Spain, or many another cathedral town all over Europe.

"Who will it be?"

"I want it to be Hodge."

"Hodge is your brother!"

"Wooden head, that's why I want it to be Hodge."

"I'm going to say Perkin."

"Perkin is too little."

"What do you mean I'm too little?"

"You have to step on somebody's back just to climb up on the chair."

"Well, you're so fat, your"—and the little boy used a hearty middle English word to denote that part of the body fashioned by the creator for embarrassment—"would split the sides of it."

"Or he'd get stuck!"

"We'd have to get Jack the smith to bring his crow to work him loose."

"Boys!" snapped the choirmaster, with as severe a look as he could muster, which was not so severe either. For this was a merry feast.

After Mass, three hundred worshipers, men and women and children, gathered outside of the cathedral door, while Bishop Simon, with his French accent, called out, "Alors, whom do we shoose for my successeur?" The people laughed as the boys cried out, "Perkin Watkins!" "Hodge the Fletcher's son!" "Nicholas of the Ford!" and so on.

Bishop Simon noted the names and then repeated them one by one, asking the boys to cheer the one whom they approved. When they had gone through them all, he paused, and intoned in his most solemn way:

"Episcopus innocentium Petrus Valtocinsis sit!"

A moment's thought—then, "It's Perkin, it's Perkin Watkins! Hurrah for Perkin, for Bishop Perkin!" And the small boy with the tart tongue, grinning and blushing, strode up to Bishop Simon, who took the miter from his head and placed it on the boy's, where it sank to the bridge of his nose, and handed him his crozier, which was twice as tall as the child.

"Wear it well, little Peter," said the bishop.

That evening at vespers, during the *Magnificat*, when they came to the words *he has cast down the mighty from their thrones, and has lifted up the lowly*, Bishop Simon descended from his seat, and the season's boy-bishop ascended it.

In the bishop's rooms

It was a few days later, and Simon had summoned Boy-bishop Perkin to his study. The boy had never seen so many books in his life; there must have been forty or fifty, bound in leather, many with gilt edging, and illuminated by the precise and prayerful hands of monk-artists whose names we will never know.

"Pierre-ken," said Simon, "you have led matins and vespers most impressively. Your voice rings like a bell. How is it," he said, trying to size up the boy-bishop, "that you know the part of the priest so well?"

"I've heard it many times, Lord, since I was small."

"Since," said Simon, smiling. "How many years do you have, Pierre-ken?"

"I am eleven," said the boy.

"Almost too late," said Simon, "but perhaps not. I'm thinking you can read. Is it true?"

"I can read a little, Lord," and the boy glanced toward the books.

"You can read the English words?"

"Yes, Lord."

"Who taught you to do so?"

The boy hesitated. "No one, Lord. I mean, I sometimes asked people who knew, and they told me what the word said, and from there I figured it out myself. My father reads a little."

"And you can read the French words?"

"If I know what they mean, Lord."

Simon's eyes shone with merriment. "Ah, but we say not prayers in the English or the French. Can you read the Lateen?"

"I think so. A little."

"Bring me that book on my table," said Simon. He opened it to a page embellished with red and blue and gold figures, and a large initial I, made into the form of Christ, ruler of all, with his hand extended in blessing. Perkin had seen such a book before, but never this way—facing it, touching it, peering into it. "Read the first words on this page, if it please you," said Simon.

The boy stared hard, then suddenly brightened. He knew what it said. He had heard it many times before. "*In principio erat Verbum*," he called out, beaming.

"*In principio erat Verbum*," said Simon. "Would you like to learn to read the rest, Perkin? Would you like to learn the wisdom that is in all these books?"

It was like asking the boy if he would like to sail the seas, or search an endless cave for gold. "Yes, Lord," he said.

"We will see to it," said Simon.

"My father is not a rich man, Lord," said Perkin.

"That is no matter."

Learning to wield the crozier

So for the twenty-two days between Saint Nicholas' Day and Holy Innocents, Peter Watkins, called Perkin, was the boy-bishop of Salisbury. He led the cathedral choir in lauds and matins and vespers. He intoned the bishop's part in the *Angelus*. He did not confer the sacraments, of course, but he was granted the authority to correct his fellow choristers informally, and when he walked about the streets with the miter and crozier, the people of Salisbury smiled and greeted him, asking how his Lordship was, and offering him some sweetmeat if he were hungry, which, as he was a growing lad, he always was.

One time Boy-bishop Perkin came upon a couple of boys shouting and pounding one another in the street. He strode into their midst with the crozier and used it as a fence to keep them apart. "What's this foolishness?" he said, in the most imperious voice he could assume. When one of the boys dared to reply with a word that it is best not to repeat, his Lordship, with two hands, slammed the base of the crozier down on the malefactor's foot, much to the momentary delight of his opponent—who was soon checked in his mirth by a straight look from Perkin.

"Bishop Pierre-kin," said Simon to him later that day, "I have something to say to you. Do you know what that crozier is for?"

"It's a shepherd's staff, my Lord," said Perkin. "It's like what our shepherds bring with them out in the fields."

"And why do they do that, Pierre-kin?" said Simon. "Do they bring their staves so that they may quarrel with one another, like brainless boys?"

Perkin blushed. "No, Lord. They bring them in case of wolves."

"They bring them in case of wolves. Then why, my son, do I carry a crozier?"

Perkin was silent.

"Is it because I wish to use it like a club, against my children?"

"No, Lord."

"Then why do I carry a crozier?"

Perkin cocked his head. The truth came to him in a flash. "In case of wolves."

"Yes, in case of wolves. Come, Pierre-ken, and let me tell you about the wolves, and how the shepherd keeps them from the flock."

Solemn and merry

On the feast of the Innocents, Perkin resigned his office and gave the miter and crozier back to Bishop Simon. So it was each year, with each boy-bishop.

For God has chosen the weak of the world to confound the strong, and the foolish to confound the wise: for the foolishness of God is wiser than men. *Father, creator of heaven and earth,* said Jesus, *I give you thanks and praise, because you have hidden these things from the wise and prudent of this world, and have revealed them to babes.*

It's good for us to feast and to be merry, because all mankind was dead and has now been brought again to life; we were lost, and now we are found. A babe in a manger struck terror into the heart of Herod the Great, and justly so; and one itinerant preacher in Galilee would overcome the massive might of the Roman Empire.

So there is always something of the carnival near to Christian worship: something of mirth, that boisterous country-cousin of joy. The Church paints in bold and bright colors. Her very solemnity is near to a paradise of song.

We have no idea how many of the boy-bishops became bishops indeed, or priests, or monks, or solid men of faith in their villages. I'd wager it was quite a few.

We might ask why our medieval forebears could do so bold a thing, which for us moderns would seem unthinkable. Perhaps we might recover some of that spirit of mirth? A gift not to be spurned!

এ৩ এ৩ এ৩

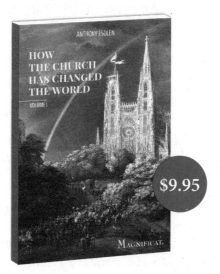

MAGNIFICAT®

Hear it from Our Readers...

I have never written anything to the MAGNIFICAT *but I felt I should.*

I have been an avid monthly user/reader for many years! Without this monthly reading I don't know what I would do. This is my daily and nightly link to our Lord that I rely on so much...and I tell all my friends.

The meditations, reflections, and readings are my food for the day and sometimes the week....

I hope you and everyone involved with MAGNIFICAT *realize how much so many people depend on every word that's written.*

DAVE

Today when I gave Jim a copy of MAGNIFICAT, *he looked at me and said, "Lisa, aside from bringing me the Eucharist, of all the things you have done for me, sharing* MAGNIFICAT *is the best gift you've given me."*

Jim knows he may have very little time left here on earth. Nonetheless, he told me today that he is going to get a one-year subscription! Praise God! That's thanks to the beautiful work that everyone at MAGNIFICAT *does!*

LISA

I cannot tell you how much MAGNIFICAT *has ministered to us at every phase of our family's journey with Christ, including the joys and sorrows. We have found our daily treasure in the words of Scripture, the lives of the Saints, the commentaries, and every single word of* MAGNIFICAT. *We are truly a family attached to our* MAGNIFICAT.

BETH

www.magnificat.com or call 1-866-273-5215